JOSEPHINE CLARDY FOX

Josephine age one.

Josephine Clardy Fox
(Portrait by R. Hinton Perry, 1915)

JOSEPHINE CLARDY FOX

Traveler, Opera-Goer,
Collector of Art,
Benefactor

by

RUBY BURNS

EL PASO

TEXAS WESTERN PRESS

1973

Library of Congress Catalog Card Number 73-83925

ISBN 0-87404-042-6

CHAPTERS

PHOTOGRAPHS

INTRODUCTION

SOON AFTER THE DEATH of Mrs. Josephine Clardy Fox May 11, 1970, the entire El Paso Community felt a deep sense of gratitude upon learning that this generous lady had made a magnificent bequest of her entire estate to The University of Texas at El Paso. Not long afterward, it was decided that an initial gesture of our profound indebtedness to Mrs. Fox would be to gather all possible information about her life and works and to record these facts in printed form.

We felt most fortunate to obtain the consent of Mrs. Ruby Burns to undertake this task, which proved to be not only challenging, but at times, I am confident she would agree, elusive and difficult. During her life, Mrs. Fox remained a distinctly private person, and it required a great deal of initiative and imagination on the part of her biographer to track down even the essential chronology of her life.

Mrs. Burns, a journalist of long experience and a facile writer, has captured, I believe, the spirit, the manifold interests and endeavors of this remarkable woman. She has diligently followed every lead and clue to arrive at the story of the life of Josephine Clardy Fox, whose benefaction to The University of Texas at El Paso will assure that her memory will live as long as the institutions of society survive. It is my hope that her memory will be honored in other appropriate ways, in addition to the publication of her biography. Her abiding interest in the arts, well documented here, might prove a guiding factor in some future manner of honoring her.

On behalf of the University which I served as President at the time of her death, I should like to record here once again our deepest sense of gratitude for the confidence in the institution represented by the splendid benefaction of Josephine Clardy Fox. Her gift to our University will have an incalculable effect for good in all the years that lie ahead.

JOSEPH R. SMILEY
President Emeritus
H. Y. Benedict Professor Modern Languages

El Paso, Texas
September, 1973

Dr. and Mrs. Joseph R. Smiley in the Hoover House with paintings, urns and books from the Clardy Fox collection.

Unusual oak vitrines in Louis XVI style holding fine Limoges enamels and a small Roza oil painting.

Sevres clock and matching candlesticks in reception room of Hoover House, the pieces dating to 1780.

Josephine and Her Mother, 1912

CHAPTER I

So Rich, So Poor

JOSEPHINE CLARDY FOX HAD AWAKENED that May morning in 1943 with a headache and a nagging pain in her back that had bothered her ever since her injury in an automobile accident several years ago. She had risen early and fixed herself a cup of tea in the small upstairs kitchen near her bedroom and, after taking a pain pill, had fallen asleep again.

Awake again, feeling better but still afraid the pain would return if she got up, she lay there, thinking about her mother. She had lived alone since her mother's death in 1940. Whenever she thought of her mother, a great loneliness seized her. Somehow, she did not miss her husband, Eugene, as she did her "Little Mama," Allie Clardy. Some people might think it strange, she realized, for a middle-aged woman like herself to be so attached to her mother that she grieved more for her than for the husband to whom she had been married for almost twenty years.

But Mama was always with me, she thought, *and before he died, Gene was away so much on railroad business that I got accustomed to his absence. Oh, those dreadful last few years of his life, when he was suffering so much mental anguish. Maybe things would have been different if I had stayed by his side instead of leaving him to face his troubles alone.*

But these thoughts were painful, and Josephine forced herself to dismiss them. She began to think about her brilliant lawyer-father, Zeno B. Clardy. He had been dead more than 40 years now, she mused, and at times it was difficult for her to recall his face clearly. But she did remember well what a kind, patient father he had been. Indulgent, too. He wanted his little girl to have whatever would make her happy. For instance, there was the time when she wanted so badly to take a holiday trip to Mexico City; although she was not quite sixteen, he had let her go. She was chaperoned, of course, by an older friend, Miss King, and they had letters of introduction to various business friends of her father's in Mexico. Even so, both her parents back in El Paso were almost frantic with worry until they received her letter saying she had arrived safely and was having a wonderful time. Father had sent money and then Mother slipped in twice as much without his knowledge. Yes, they had been indulgent parents, all right.

That winter, they enrolled her in a finishing school, Hosmer Hall in St. Louis, and Mother went along to get her settled. Mother was still there when Christmas came and poor little Papa had to spend lonely days and nights in El Paso.

Josephine liked school, especially the classes in drama and music, and she could recall how exciting it was when the drama teacher announced that she was to have a part in the school play at the end of the year. Most of the other girls were seniors or juniors and it was just heavenly for a lowly sophomore to be in the play. She was cast as Jacques, a lord attending the banished Duke, in Shakespeare's *As You Like It*. Rehearsals and fittings for the costumes filled every spare moment, and she loved it all. She and the other girls had become great friends; it was like belonging to a secret society from which the rest of the world was shut out.

Then came the night of the performance. She remembered the stage fright that seized her when it was time to make her entrance. Her mouth went dry, her knees felt as if they would buckle and her hands shook, but somebody gave her a push and she found herself out on the stage, blinded by a great white light.

Somehow she began to speak the familiar lines in a voice that seemed to come from outside herself. Then one of her friends in the cast whispered that she was doing fine and all at once it was just as if it were another rehearsal and she forgot her fear. Father said afterward that he had never been so proud of anybody in his whole life.

She had kept the clipping from the St. Louis paper about the play and had read it many times. The story began:

Strains of music and ripples of applause from the company gathered in the brilliantly-lighted portion of the lawn of the Kauffman mansion . . . drew attention last night to a stage built among the trees upon which the pupils of Hosmer Hall presented to an appreciative audience "As You Like It." A more fascinating scene could scarcely have been fashioned than this open-air performance upon a stage which was, perhaps, a fair counterpart of the one on which the play was first given.

Seated in front of this stage in the sylvan theatre that had been arranged by placing chairs about the lawn were 300 guests, either parents or friends of the players. Calcium lights were placed back of the audience, throwing a bright light upon the stage. The splendid lawn was illuminated by the mellow light of the Chinese lanterns. The costumes worn were rich, and the bright light thrown upon them heightened their beauty.

Floral offerings were features of every act, following the applause of the guests which brought the players to the front of the stage. Some of these floral tributes were magnificent bouquets of American Beauties. The affair partook of the nature of a commencement exercise, but there was an interest in the work done on the stage not found in the ordinary graduating exercises.

Josephine in Shakespearean costume
at Hosmer Hall, age 18 years.

Her love of the theatre, born that night, continued and she had witnessed many brilliant performances on stages in New York, Chicago, San Francisco, London and other world capitals. By donation and attendance she had supported drama and music in El Paso and elsewhere all her life.

The school years had passed quickly and then Father came to St. Louis for the last time. He needed to see her Uncle Firmin Desloge on business and he would take Josephine back home with him. Mother was ill and could not accompany him. Uncle Firmin and Aunt Lydia, who was Mama's sister, had a big house and they often invited her there for parties. They had been lovely, too, about introducing her to the young people of St. Louis and including her in family dinners, excursions on the river, or other fun events.

At the end of school, there had been so much gaiety! She was on the go constantly with her Hosmer Hall friends, her beaux and her cousins (there were Clardy cousins, too, in St. Louis) whom she hated to leave. She was a real beauty in those days, with her dark hair, dark eyes, creamy complexion and tall, willowy figure. Everybody talked about how beautiful she was and Father had beamed with pride and said, "She looks like her mother."

That spring of 1901 had been beautiful in St. Louis. There was a Desloge family picnic for Josephine and Mr. Clardy in Forest Park, where the fresh green of the grass and the shade of tall trees created a wonderful setting. Father and Uncle Firmin sat on a bench and talked business after supper, while she and Aunt Lydia packed up the remnants of food and the servants carried the baskets to the carriages. Josephine and her handsome cousin, Firmin, Jr., strolled through the trees while he regaled her with his exploits of his first year away at college. His fourteen-year-old brother Joseph made a nuisance of himself throwing rocks at the birds until his mother decided it was time to go home.

As the carriage rolled away from the park, Father had pointed out to her the house on Olive Street where he had stayed as a young bachelor while attending law school at Washington University. Back at her boarding house, she finished packing her trunk, for she and Father were to take the train for El Paso the next day.

She was just twenty then and the whole world for Josephine was carefree and full of happiness. But all that changed a few days later when, back in El Paso, Father had suffered a heart attack and died.

It was an almost unbearable shock to his wife and daughter, both of whom adored the quiet, unassuming head of the household. He was so young, just 45, and had seemed so well, so full of life on the last day he lived, that Allie could not believe the cruel fact of his death. She and Josephine clung to each other and wept, while kind neighbors came in to help the stricken pair. Then, clad in deep mourning, Zeno Clardy's wife and only child attended his funeral. It was conducted by ministers of the Christian and Presbyterian churches. Members of the Bar Association and Woodmen of the World paid their respects by attending in a body. This man's integrity and high principles had won the respect and love of the community, whose leaders paid him tribute at the last rite. Pallbearers were Mayor B. F. Hammett, Major R. H. R. Loughborough, Dr. J. B. Brady, A. P. Coles, M. B. Davis and E. V. Berrien, active; W. H. Burges Jr., Judge T. A. Falvey, W. W. Turney, Judge Peyton Edwards, Judge William Buckler and Wyndham Kemp, honorary.

All that was long ago. Now, as Josephine roused from her reverie, she suddenly realized that she was very hungry. It was nearly noon and there was not a morsel of food in the house. *If Mother were alive,* she thought, *she would not let things like this happen.* Mama had been a good cook herself, but she almost always had a hired cook presiding in the big kitchen downstairs and the pantry was kept full of provisions.

With a smile, Josephine remembered the Chinese cook, whom all the neighbor children adored, for he had always treated them with litche nuts and other small delicacies. This brought to her mind Jane Davis, the little girl next door, who used to run in and out of the Clardy house, especially the kitchen. She decided to call Jane, now the wife of Major Dick McMaster, and ask her to bring some food.

Jane answered the phone promptly. "What are you and Dick having for lunch today?" Josephine asked. "And could you spare some for me? I am here all alone, sick in bed, and have nothing in the house to eat." Of course she would come and bring Josephine some food, Jane said. "But how will I get into that fortress you live in?" she asked. The big house on Montana Avenue really did have the look of an impregnable fort, with iron grilles at the shuttered windows and heavy locks at the doors, all installed following a burglary years earlier.

Josephine said she would drop a key on a string to the front door from the upstairs balcony. A little later, Jane arrived bearing a tray of food, found the key and climbed the stairs to Josephine's bedroom. Here she found her friend lying in bed, wearing a lace-trimmed negligee over her nightdress and several diamond bracelets on her arm.

Although the youthful beauty had long since faded, there was still something striking about Josephine, Jane thought. Abundant dark hair framed her face and hung down about her shoulders. Her skin was still creamy and unblemished. But her eyes now were constantly hidden behind dark glasses, for one of them had an ugly scar across the surface and there was no vision left in it. Jane did not know what had happened but she had heard that a surgeon tried to remove a small growth and infection had followed. Josephine and her family blamed him for the disfigurement and loss of sight. It all had happened years earlier, either in New York or Europe, where the frantic Josephine had travelled far and wide seeking a doctor who could save or restore her sight.[1] The damage to the eye was tragically beyond repair, but there was a greater tragedy, an injury to the spirit of the young woman from which she never recovered. Her eyes had been one of her loveliest features, large brown orbs so soulful that young men were often transfixed by their gaze.

Josephine liked the attentions of these young men. She loved to flirt; in fact, she had kept Eugene Fox waiting for more than ten years of courtship while she carried on little flirtations with other men.

After the loss of her eye, Josephine seemed to lose some of the sweetness that had characterized her as a young girl. She would never discuss the loss and friends dared not ask her about it. Black moods now came over her at times and fits of temper caused her to lash out at whatever person or thing crossed her path.[2]

Today, however, Josephine was in one of her better moods and she and Jane chatted pleasantly while she ate her lunch. Jane wondered why her friend wore the diamond bracelets in bed, not realizing that to Josephine they were a symbol of security. Although those times were gone now, Josephine could not forget the long, hard years through which she and her mother had suffered, trying desperately

[1] Another close friend, Frances Vance Durling, recalls that the eye injury occurred in New York while Josephine was a music student there. She and her mother were walking past a construction site when a particle of metal or other material struck Josephine's eye.

[2] Chris Fox, a former El Paso sheriff and now a bank officer, recalls that when he was about 10 years old he and a neighbor boy had decided to earn some spending money by selling lemonade. So they set up a little stand on the sidewalk in front of the Clardy home. About the time they were ready for business, the enterprise came to an abrupt halt. Josephine swept out of her front door, a commanding figure in long dress covered with a duster and wearing a big hat held on by a veil. A horse-drawn hack had been ordered from the livery stable and she carried a light whip in her hand. Spying the boys and their miserable little stand on her sidewalk, she cried, "You little rascals, get away from my house!" and raising the whip, she appeared ready to use it on them. Mr. Fox says they fled in terror, knocking over the stand and lemonade as they went.

to hold the properties Mr. Clardy had purchased before his death and often finding themselves, during the depression years, on the verge of losing everything. When times began to turn better, Josephine bought diamonds and fine art objects. In fits of almost compulsive buying, she added to the collections her mother had started.

Diamonds speak the language of love to the unloved and they whisper "we are always here" to the lonely. Thus it was not strange that Josephine found comfort in her bracelets, or that, many years later when she was to spend long weeks and months in the hospital, she took some of her jewels with her.

Having finished her lunch, Josephine thanked Jane for bringing it and then asked, "Darling, did you notice anything new downstairs as you came up?" For the life of her, Jane could not recall seeing anything new, for the house was filled to overflowing with fine tables, chairs, vitrines and cabinets holding Meissen, Dresden, Sevres and all sorts of art objects. Collections crowded each other for space in every nook and cranny, so Jane had to admit that she had not noticed anything new.

"Well, my dear, you just must see it as you go out," Josephine said. "It is in a glass case on the ormolu table at the foot of the stairs, a gorgeous fan that belonged to the Empress Eugenie. It came just this week and I simply adore it. My good friend, Lucinda Templin, found it for me in California and had it sent on to me. You know, she has excellent taste and she finds some beautiful things for me every now and again when she is travelling."

Jane prepared to leave. *Poor Josie,* she thought, *lots of diamonds and a house full of treasures, but nobody to love and nothing to eat. How dreadful to be so rich, yet so poor!*

Allie Davis Clardy in her bridal dress

Zeno B. Clardy, 1880

CHAPTER II

Early Days

◆§ JOSEPHINE'S FATHER, Zeno Blanks Clardy, got his unusual name from his mother's family. He was the son of John E. Clardy and his wife Lydia, a member of the Blanks family, with whom "Zeno" was a popular Christian name. They lived in the village of Liberty-ville, near the town of Farmington in St. Francois County, Southeast Missouri, where John was a farmer and dry goods merchant. When their first child was born in 1856, John and Lydia named him Zeno Blanks. He grew up with two brothers and three sisters: Johnson and Willis; Susan, Sally, and Fanny.

Zeno attended local schools and began his study of law in the office of his uncle, Martin L. Clardy, a distinguished lawyer of Southeast Missouri, whose wife was the daughter of a prominent citizen of Farmington. Martin had served as a cavalry officer in the Confederate Army and after the war had formed a law partnership with Judge William Carter. For many years, Carter and Clardy was a leading law firm in Southeast Missouri.

Martin Clardy was elected to Congress as a Democrat and served for five consecutive terms. He was a "warm and devoted friend of President McKinley."[1] After retiring from Congress he returned to Farmington to resume the practice of law. Later he was appointed general attorney and vice president of the Missouri Pacific Railroad with headquarters in St. Louis.

According to a biographical sketch in the Cape Girardeau *Daily Republican* which appeared at the time of his death in 1914, Martin Clardy served with distinction in this latter position and he was known nationally for his fairness and efficiency in the settlement of claims and disputes in railroad matters.

Young Zeno Clardy was graduated from Washington University in St. Louis in 1876 with the LL. B. degree which entitled him to admission to the bar of the State and U. S. Courts. His home address was

[1] From biographical material in archives of Missouri Historical Society, St. Louis.

Farmington, Missouri. While attending the University he lived at 1407 Olive Street, where he "undoubtedly paid $25 to $35 per month for good board and lodging," according to Miss Erna Arndt, registrar of Washington University Law School.

Zeno had completed the two-year course in one year. He returned to Farmington at once to begin the practice of law. Not long afterward, he met the young lady who was to be his bride, Miss Allie Davis.

Allie was the youngest of five daughters of Col. Joseph Davis and his wife, the former Rebecca Nave. These five were the only surviving children of a family of three boys and seven girls. The others died in infancy or early childhood.

The Davis family lived across the state of Missouri from St. Louis, not far by train from Kansas City. Their farm home was five miles from the town of Lexington, and they used the mail address of Walker, Missouri. Colonel Davis had been a man of substantial means and owner of a large number of slaves when the Civil War broke out: He chose the cause of the South and fought under Gen. Sterling Price of the Confederate Army. The close of the war found Joseph Davis in Austin, Texas, his slaves and property gone, with life to begin anew. He returned to Missouri and settled on the farm in Lafayette County, near Lexington, where Allie was born on November 2, 1865.

Colonel Davis rebuilt his fortunes; he became prominent in Lafayette County and was well known in the state from 1865 until his death in 1902. His wife died in 1907.

Allie probably was visiting in the home of her sister Lydia and husband, Firmin Desloge, in St. Louis when she and Zeno Clardy met. She was very young, very innocent and deliciously pretty. Zeno's fate was sealed. He fell madly in love with the young girl from Lexington and immediately besieged her with a flood of letters, begging her to set the wedding date. Allie's parents doubtless thought her much too young to marry; they sent her off to Colorado to spend several months with another married sister. Upon her return, she and Zeno became engaged and the wedding was set for the autumn of that year, 1880.

In the meantime, the young attorney was making his mark in his home territory of St. Francois County. That summer he decided to run for the office of prosecuting attorney. His letters to Allie tell of an arduous campaign with many speaking engagements, from which he emerged exhausted but flushed with victory.

He wrote to Allie on Aug. 18: "I will advise you, certainly, of the results of the election. In the towns of St. Joe and Desloge, there's quite an excitement over my race. Before Mr. C. withdrew, every saloon with two exceptions in the County, was for him. I WOULD SUFFER DEFEAT before sacrificing principle."

Later in August he wrote from Libertyville: "I am fully satisfied with my attempts heretofore — I have accidentally (I suppose) succeeded beyond my greatest expectations. Last night at the meeting our audience numbered about 300 and when I finished there were 'three cheers for Clardy!' and I was the only one of about five speakers thus honored."

During the campaign, word came from Austin, Texas, where his family had gone, that his mother was gravely ill. His father wrote that the doctor had thought she might die and he had sent for Zeno's sister Sallie, who was in Dallas at the time. But Zeno wrote Allie: "Thanks to that Great Physician, she is much better — is spared to us all. In every letter she writes me, she sends love to Allie and asks me to come soon."

The wedding of Allie Davis and Zeno Clardy took place at 4 p.m. on October 4, 1880, in the farm home of the bride's parents. Zeno arrived by train early the day before the wedding, accompanied by his uncle Harve, who was to perform the ceremony. They had a whole day to pace the streets of a strange town and Zeno, a nervous and anxious bridegroom, found the time passed slowly indeed. He had hoped Allie would come to Lexington and spend some time with him during that long day, but she declined. It would not seem proper, and besides, there were too many preparations for the exciting event to be made at home.

In his last letter to Allie before the wedding, Zeno wondered who would be present for the ceremony. His parents, of course, could not attend because of his mother's illness; also his uncle Martin was ill and would not be present. He asked if her sister Lydia and Mr. Desloge would be there. He said he feared they would have preferred some other suitor to himself, but that he planned to be friendly to them and hoped they would come to approve of him after he was in the family. He did not know how large the crowd would be for the ceremony, but he said, "Even if there are a thousand people there, you will let me kiss you, won't you?"

Zeno took his bride to live in Farmington, where they had a big house with a flower and vegetable garden and a barn. Their honeymoon trip was to Texas, where Zeno proudly introduced Allie to his parents and friends. They did not stay long, for he had to be back in Farmington for the opening of the court session on November 1.

In the following year, Attorney Clardy and his wife became the parents of their only child, a little girl whom they named Josephine Marsalis. She was born in Liberty Township on August 13, 1881, when her mother was not quite 16 years old.

In April, 1882, Allie took the baby and went to visit her parents, both of whom were ill. Zeno accompanied them to St. Louis and saw them off there. Then he began to write daily letters telling Allie how terribly lonely he was and how empty the house seemed. He was planting a garden and looking after the chickens. "We have two hens with 7 chickens — 3½ to each hen," he said. In every letter he sent kisses to Josephine, whom he sometimes called by the pet name of "Jinkie." He bemoaned the fact that the piano was closed and the little buggy was in the parlor. In one letter he said, "I bought a horse today. I shall send it to pasture until you get home."

The Methodists held a revival and Zeno attended, although he was a member of the Christian Church. He wrote Allie the names of those who went up each night, to ask for prayers or to join the church, and said they might join either the Christian or the Methodist, but that most of them were joining the Methodist Church.

He mentioned also that a court session was coming up soon at St. Genevieve, where he was to be the prosecutor. Perhaps Allie would want to stay with her parents until he got back home from court, especially since they were still not well.

Allie's parents got better and she and her sisters returned to their homes. One might suppose that the tranquility and domestic bliss of the Zeno Clardy family in their Farmington home would continue for many years. The bliss may have continued, but the setting soon changed drastically. Zeno Clardy is listed as prosecuting attorney for the years 1881 to 1885 in the *Authentic History of St. Francois County* by Tom Miles. But he did not serve out the term. Before the end of 1882, Attorney Clardy and his family had arrived in El Paso, Texas. Here Zeno, Allie and Josephine were to live out their lives.

What may have impelled young Zeno Clardy to give up his promising career in Southeast Missouri and come to the frontier town of El Paso, we do not know. There were several Missourians already in El Paso and reports must have gone back about the boom that the railroads had brought when they arrived in 1881. The population of El Paso was only 700 before the arrival of the Southern Pacific in May, 1881, but a month later it had doubled. Then came the Santa Fe and the next year, the Texas and Pacific established regular passenger service from Fort Worth to El Paso. In 1881 the Mexican Central Railroad began construction at Paso del Norte (soon to change its name to Juarez) on a line that would link the border town with Mexico City. From a small village of adobe huts, El Paso began to grow by leaps and bounds, so that when the Clardys arrived, lumber and brick buildings were being constructed and "land changed hands almost faster than the recorders could write," according to C. L. Sonnichsen.[2] In the fall of 1882 Sylvester Watts of St. Louis inaugurated a municipal water system; electricity was to arrive in 1883 and in 1884 Zach White and Major W. J. Fewell were to organize a gas company.

It is possible that Zeno Clardy read some of the boomtown news in copies of El Paso newspapers, for two weeklies had rushed into print on the same day in April 1882, The El Paso *Times* and El Paso *Herald*. The State National Bank had opened for business in 1881 and by 1882 there was actually a streetcar line, a little open car drawn by a mule.

Firmin Desloge, husband of Allie's sister, Lydia, must have been infected with frontier fever as he, too, heard the stories of what was happening in El Paso. He was engaged in operating a huge lead-mining business and could not consider pulling up stakes himself to go West. However, he was willing to trust a large sum of money to Zeno Clardy for real estate investment in the booming frontier town. And so, when the Clardys arrived in El Paso, Zeno set up a law office and at once began the purchase of land for the Desloge and Clardy real estate firm.

Firmin Desloge had grown up in St. Francois County, said to be one of the richest lead-mining areas of the world. His father, a native of France, kept a general store there during the Civil War. Lead mining in that region was conducted then by individual owners. These small-time miners would take their ore to the store to trade for mer-

2 C. L. Sonnichsen, *Pass of the North* (El Paso: Texas Western Press, 1968), p. 225.

chandise. The store owner obtained from them options on land, thus making possible the family's beginning in lead mining. When the Desloge Consolidated Lead Co., headed by Firmin, was sold in 1929, its stockholders realized about eighteen million dollars. Firmin Desloge died later that year at the age of 86, survived by Lydia and their two sons, Firmin V. and Joseph.

In 1933 the Firmin Desloge Hospital, a 15-story building, was dedicated in St. Louis to his memory, half of the cost donated by Mrs. Desloge and her sons. The hospital is now owned jointly by St. Louis University and the Sisters of Mercy. The Sisters still operate the hospital which from the outset was devoted to the care of the needy. A large percentage of its services are still given without charge or at fees less than cost.

When Zeno Clardy arrived in El Paso, he was accepted as a law partner by Allan Blacker, a respected member of the legal fraternity. Some of the other prominent citizens that he met on arrival were Joseph Magoffin, James P. Hague, Solomon and Joseph Schutz, James A. Tays, Charles R. Morehead, O. T. Bassett, Ynocente Ochoa, Mariano Samaniego, W. W. Mills, W. M. Coldwell, W. H. Austin, Dr. Hugh White, Llewellyn Davis, William Rheinheimer, Dr. Walter Vilas, James H. White, Adolf Krakauer, Simeon H. Newman, T. A. Falvey, William S. Hills, Jacob Calisher, and James L. Marr.

El Paso was a wide-open town in 1882, with saloons on every corner and in between. The big saloons all had gambling tables in the back and these were full every night. Some of these establishments offered "girls and gaiety;" some had vaudeville acts and brass bands that paraded the streets to drum up trade just before the show started. Down on Utah Street (which is now South Mesa) there was a row of bordellos where the conduct of the "filles publiques" was arousing the indignation of the respectable people of the town, according to S. H. Newman, editor of the *Lone Star*. Shootings were frequent and a famous frontier marshal, Dallas Stoudenmire, met his death in 1882 as a result of his feud with the Manning Brothers.

Mr. Clardy had a profitable legal business and it is said that he acquired much valuable property in lieu of money as legal fees. When, after a few years, Judge Blacker was forced to retire from the firm for reasons of health, Mr. Clardy became associated with Attorney H. H. Neill.

{14}

In the meantime, the chubby little Josephine was nearing school age. Her parents lived in a big frame house at the corner of Mesa and Wyoming (this location now being part of the depressed freeway). They sent Josephine to a parochial school, the Academy of the Immaculate Conception, operated by the Sisters of Mercy. Her report card at the end of the year 1890 has been preserved and shows that she made perfect marks in each of ten subjects.

She entered the public schools in 1891 and was in the fourth grade at Mesa School when she was nine. She moved on to the Old Central School for the eighth grade in 1894-95. Afterwards, her parents sent her to St. Louis to attend the exclusive girls' school, Hosmer Hall.

In 1893 Josephine's father made an unsuccessful bid to be named U. S. Consul in Juarez. He had endorsements from many prominent men in Missouri, including senators and congressmen, whose aid had been solicited by Colonel Davis and possibly by Martin Clardy also. Prominent men in Juarez, Chihuahua City and Mexico City also wrote to endorse him, but Mr. Clardy did not receive the appointment.

Among the El Pasoans with whom the Clardys made friends soon after their arrival were Judge and Mrs. James P. Hague. When the Southern Pacific's first train reached El Paso in 1881, a big celebration was held. Public-spirited citizens built a pavilion, bunting decorated buildings, spectators thronged the streets, and leading citizens, arrayed in top hats and Prince Albert coats, awaited the arrival of the distinguished railroad officials, including the president of the line, C. F. Crocker.

Judge Falvey introduced Judge Blacker, who welcomed the guests in polished phrases that glowed with predictions for a glorious future for El Paso. The Governor of Texas had told him that if he were a young man, he would settle in El Paso "with the firm belief that it would be within his power to become a millionaire — that El Paso is the best place in the United States to make a fortune in a single lifetime."[3]

After more speeches, a procession was formed and the group moved to the hall over Schutz's store, where the principal part of the program got under way. The ladies joined the assemblage here, attired in their finest silks and wearing their diamonds and other ornaments. Here Judge Hague, "No mean maker of speeches, achieved the pinnacle of

3 Sonnichsen, p. 228.

his oratorial career."[4] He too saw a glorious future for El Paso. He had every right to make the principal speech, for he had donated 30 acres of land in the heart of town to the Southern Pacific, so that the trains could be brought right into the business district. A banquet that night was held in the Central Hotel and a grand ball in Schutz's Hall followed, with music by the best Mexican band from Paso del Norte across the river.

Attorney James Hague had arrived in El Paso in 1871 after an arduous stagecoach journey from Austin, Texas, to take up his duties as the first district attorney of El Paso. He had been appointed to the post by Governor E. J. Davis shortly after being admitted to the bar at age 21. Returning later to Austin to be married, he brought his bride Flora here by stagecoach and they bought their first home in ·1873 from Louis Cardis. It was a large adobe house of many rooms occupying a square block on Santa Fe and San Francisco Streets. Here they were to rear a family of eight children, the daughter Clara being about the same age as Josephine Clardy.[5]

Young Josephine Clardy probably enjoyed many happy hours playing with Clara and her sisters and brothers in that big house inside the adobe walls. Perhaps she sat in school with Clara, as both were taught by the Sisters and dutifully learned their catechism together. The Hague family were devout Catholics; the Clardys were members of the Christian (or Church of Christ) denomination, but this made little if any difference to the children.

Josephine and Clara formed a close friendship that lasted as long as they lived. Josephine also knew the other sisters and brothers very well. The Hague sons and daughters were Kate, the eldest, who became Mrs. Howard L. Laubach; Philip; Lillian (Mrs. Corcoran); Clara, who never married; Jim, living in 1971 in California; Aileen

4 Ibid, p. 229.

5 Another daughter, Lillian, who became Mrs. Tom Corcoran, writing in *Password* in 1956, says of the Hague home: "It was a showplace and a rendezvous for the young and old of El Paso. The rambling old adobe place seemed to suit my mother and father's purpose for a happy family life . . . with a beautiful orchard, cottonwood and chinaberry trees and a brown, muddy stream of water called an 'aceque' running down the road right in front of the place. It was completely enclosed by high adobe walls that gave us a feeling of protection when the gates were locked at night and as my mother said, 'there was nothing to be afraid of but Indians.' In 1878 news spread over town that Mrs. Hague had a piano, the first one in El Paso, and it took two months overland by oxen team to accomplish the perilous journey."

(Mrs. James Hill, who resides in El Paso); Juydin (Mrs. J. M. Elliott, living in Florida) and Flora (Mrs. Walter Wilson, in California.)[6]

An exciting experience for Attorney Clardy occurred in 1899 when he prosecuted a case that took him to Hawaii and brought newspaper publicity at home and in San Francisco. An article of September 5 in the San Francisco *Chronicle* reported the story dramatically:

Residents of El Paso, Texas will be interested to know that E. A. Monroe, who did business for many years [there] . . . was recently arrested in Honolulu under the name of W. D. Earl and compelled to turn over a large amount of goods which he had obtained from various wholesalers and had taken out of the country by a neat little game which he fancied would remain undiscovered. Up to last April Monroe was a thrifty and prosperous merchant in Texas, whose credit was good with the wholesale firms with whom he traded. Monroe, however, does not seem to have been satisfied with his modest gains. He planned a little stroke of business which would make him wealthy, and working toward that end bought goods freely from mercantile establishments stretching from New York to San Francisco and from Milwaukee to Richmond, Va. The goods amounted to several thousands of dollars.

Upon receiving them . . . he removed them from his store by degrees until but a few hundred dollar's worth remained. The bulk of his purchases were stored in a vacant house where they were encased in trunks labelled 'Household goods' and shipped to a consignee in San Francisco. When all of the goods had been dispatched, Monroe quietly followed to S. F., received them himself, cleared them for Honolulu and then took ship for Hawaii, sailing under the assumed name of W. D. Earl.

Several weeks after his flight from El Paso, the creditors began to suspect that something was wrong, no answer being received to their many letters. The creditors called to their assistance . . . R. G. Dun & Co. and asked the collectors to trace their man, the whereabouts of the defaulter being entirely unknown to those whom he had defrauded. Jellett and Meyerstein, attorneys for Dun in San Francisco, went to work on the case. They found out from El Paso that Monroe had shipped his goods to W. D. Earl, San Francisco, and it was soon learned that a man whose description tallied with that of Monroe had received the goods there and had later shipped them by schooner to Honolulu. He himself went to Honolulu a few days later, representing himself as a European steerage passenger.

Z. B. Clardy, an attorney of El Paso, after being apprised of these facts, left on the next steamer for Honolulu. A week or so later, accompanied by a deputy marshal, Clardy walked into Earl's place of business and greeted him familiarly as Monroe. But Earl replied that his name was not Monroe and that he had not the pleasure of the Texan's acquaintance. When asked

6 Interview, Mrs. James Hill, 1971.

if he had not been in business in El Paso he inquired where El Paso was. The deputy marshal was instructed to levy on Earl's stock and the next day, the debtor still proving obstinate, he was arrested on civil process. As soon as Monroe was in jail, he weakend and confessed his identity and his willingness to turn over all he had. The attorney returned home with the welcome news that the assets were ample to satisfy all claims.

Monroe merely asked for a pair of overalls and a blue sweater from his former stock. These were given him and he is now at work as a day laborer in Honolulu.

Allie Clardy kept two letters that Zeno wrote while in Honolulu; he attached his receipted hotel bill. He stayed at the Royal Hawaiian (which he said was the finest hotel he had ever seen), where he paid the princely sum of $3 per day! He had arrived in Honolulu on a Friday evening and learned that a big ball was in progress at the Palace. He went there to contact an attorney with whom he wished to arrange a meeting next morning. He found the attorney, but did not linger at the ball as he said he did not have his dress suit along and the others were "gorgeously arrayed." By a stroke of luck, he had seen Monroe on the street at a distance on the night of arriving and had recognized him; so he knew his man was on the scene.

Because no court was in session until Monday, Zeno had time to see something of the island and to call on El Paso friends. He wrote of Mr. and Mrs. Offley, who were "delighted to see me and asked many questions about you and Josephine." Colonel Ruhlen, whom he knew, was ill and so he did not see him; he had planned to call on President Dole, but he was visiting another island. He had been for a swim in the ocean; had seen "Queen Lil's palace and gardens" and many beautiful homes with the palms, coconuts and flowering trees. He had gone to the Union Church on Sunday morning, then home to dinner with one of his lawyers and his wife. That evening he went to church again "to my own church where I heard a good sermon and met several of the brethren."

Although enchanted with the island and its scenery, he said there is no place like home and he was anxious to get on the first steamer back. His letter, written on August 13, said: "I have not forgotten that this is Josephine's birthday. I have thought much about both of you and long to be with you." But he could not conclude his business in time to sail on the Doric Tuesday and so he had to wait for the next ship, which sailed on August 18, 1899.

CHAPTER III

The Music Student

◄§ WHEN MAJOR R. H. R. LOUGHBOROUGH came to Fort Bliss in 1899 he found the post to be a group of brick buildings located on a high mesa about five miles East of the growing village of El Paso. There was nothing else but desert, cactus and mesquite on the mesa, but there was a fine view of mountains on all sides; the air was clear and bracing and the sun shone every day.

He could not have known then how much El Paso and its people would come to mean to him. He and his wife took part in civic affairs and formed lasting friendships with the townspeople, who showed their esteem and gratitude by presenting him with a gold watch and chain when he left Fort Bliss.

The officers' quarters on the post were comfortable and spacious and Mrs. Loughborough soon made her home the center of social life at Fort Bliss. Many a young officer, stationed here far from home, found his loneliness dispelled by the dances, picnics and parties planned by Mrs. Loughborough.

Miss Josephine Clardy and other young women of the town were included in this gaiety. Mrs. L., asking one of the Negro soldiers to drive her into El Paso, would ride in a big Army vehicle drawn by a team of horses to gather a score or so of El Paso's fairest daughters and take them to the fort to a dance or party. Their mothers allowed them to go, knowing they would be well chaperoned.

Josephine became a favorite of the Loughboroughs. She often was invited to spend the night and would sometimes stay for the entire weekend. During the winter of 1900, when she was attending Hosmer Hall in St. Louis, she corresponded with them and received warm, wonderful letters from Mrs. L., who addressed her as "My dear child" and signed her letters "Mother Loughborough." In one letter she wrote of El Paso friends:

Josie Glasgow [daughter of Joseph Magoffin and wife of then Lt. Glasgow] has the dearest, prettiest little girl. The Neffs also have become fashionable with a girl! Also the [Bill] Greets, but theirs is a boy.

We had a treat the other night in hearing Miss Leonora Jackson, the violinist — she was under the auspices of the Woman's Club. In the afternoon the music department [of the club] gave her a reception at Florence, [Mrs. T. J.] Beall's. Very pretty indeed and everybody was there. She (the violinist) came late and looked dowdy, but sweet. When she began to play, you never thought of her looks or clothes. At the concert, Mrs. [Eugenia] Schuster had a box and Miss Kelley and all the girls who were with her as guests were in evening dress and looked very swell.

In another letter written in December, Mrs. L. said they had had an inspection at Fort Bliss by Captain Sibley, who brought Mrs. Sibley and their daughter, Miss Bessie, along. The Loughboroughs had entertained for them, and as usual for visitors in those days as well as today, the ladies had gone sightseeing in Juarez.

Mrs. L. said that she had invited Bessie to come back for the Mid-Winter Carnival (forerunner of the Southwestern Sun Carnival) to be in her party and she would be delighted if Josephine would join them. She said that voting for a queen of the carnival was taking place and she had heard that several of the girls had had to withdraw their names as candidates.

It is quite a public thing. The voting is by paying ten cents and so it is the most money will win. Mr. Kelley says his daughter, [Claire] may have it if it costs him three thousand dollars. We heard some one told Kate Crosby she could have it if she wished, for when Mr. Kelley spent one dollar, her father would spend two on her. However, Mrs. Crosby would not let Kate's name go in at all.

The Woman's Club will give a Century Ball New Year's Eve. There are to be a dozen epochs, each epoch designated by the costume of that time. Mine is the Huguenots. . . . The president [Mrs. J. A. Rawlings] will lead the Grand March with Major Loughborough of Fort Bliss.

I think Pat [O'Brien] must feel well tonight for he has been playing and is now singing. Mrs. O'Brien expects to return for Christmas, and maybe Pat's brother Tom will come down too. Mrs. O'Brien is so anxious for him to come and do something out here so as to be near her. He may come, though he hates to give up New York. A letter from Mrs. Dodge to Pat the other day asked him where Miss Clardy was in New York as she wished to call. Pat and the Major both join in sending their love and both join me in kindest remembrance to your mother.

Pat O'Brien and Mike Dodge, both stationed at Fort Bliss, had been friends in New York; and both admired the beautiful young Miss Clardy. Pat was suffering from tuberculosis and was not well enough to go out often, but Mike had kept company rather regularly with

Josephine before she left for St. Louis. Some of her friends thought they planned to marry and perhaps his mother had had an intimation to that effect. But Miss Clardy was not in New York that winter, so far as we know. Neither did she come home to attend the Winter Carnival, but stayed in St. Louis for the holidays. Her mother was there also, and they enjoyed the festivities with relatives and friends. What a lonely time it must have been for poor Mr. Clardy, in El Paso!

In her December letter to Josephine, Mrs. Loughborough mentioned some of the friends of the Clardys who had been to see her. Making afternoon calls was a pleasant social custom in those days. She wrote:

Myra [Newman] has been out twice to see us. Came with Lillian [Newman], then Miss Austin. I really am getting quite fond of her. If you were here, I could have you both out here often. Miss Marian Ainsa came with her Lt. and called one Sunday afternoon. Mrs. Hill brought Mrs. Beall one day and she had never been in the Garrison before.

Marian (Winkie) Ainsa and Lt. John Coulter were married later and he had a distinguished military career.[1]

Josephine corresponded at intervals that winter with Pat O'Brien, who wrote her just before Christmas, thanking her for a recent letter and sending greetings of the season. He added a sad note: "My friend, Miss Newman died in Los Angeles and I have had nothing to depress me so for years." This was Lillian, the cousin of Myra, whose death at age twenty-two saddened all her family and friends.

In April, Pat from San Pedro, Mexico, where he had gone to visit his brother at the mining camp, wrote:

I came down Saturday to see my brother and though I have an engagement to take Myra to 'look on' at the Social Club dance on Friday, my brother has invited me to remain for several dinners that will be on during Governor Ahumada's visit! He will arrive here on Friday with a mounted guard of three hundred and there will be 'doin's.' Am delighted you had the opportunity of a river trip to New Orleans, as my experience [on such a trip] was one I shall never forget. . . . I am distressed to have learned through your Mother that poor old Dick's foot has 'gone bad.' I do hope the dear fellow will not loose [sic] it or go lame.

Myra Newman and Miss McCarthy a new girl and Paul Hammett dined with us at the Post Wednesday. Miss Mc is 'a dream' and all the boys, old and young are at her feet — Emerson, Hammett, Coles, Marr etc. etc. . . .

[1] Now retired, Lt. Gen. Coulter and his wife reside in Washington, D. C.

My song will be published soon and I hope you will add it to your repertoire though it cannot rank with any of the songs you have.

I dined with your folks Friday night and your mother showed me a peach of a dress she is making. . . . Give my love to Dick[2] when you write. He never remembers me any more. Hoping you will write me again one of your delightful letters, I am, Always Yours, Patrick

After Mr. Clardy's death in 1901 his widow decided that Josephine should get away from El Paso and continue her study of music in some place where good teachers were available. For "Joe-Joe" had a rich contralto voice and, her mother believed, much musical talent. About this time a letter came from her dear friend, Mary Loughborough, whose husband, Major Loughborough, had recently been ordered to the Philippines with the Sixth Infantry. At that time his family had gone to Berkeley, California, to make their home.

"Would you like to go to Berkeley to spend the winter?" Allie asked Josephine. "There are surely fine teachers there; there will be concerts at the University and you can attend operas and plays across the bay in San Francisco." Josephine liked the idea. Her youthful spirits rose at the thought of leaving this bereaved house to be with the lively Loughboroughs again. So the plans went forward.

A suitable wardrobe had to be assembled, which meant fittings at the dressmaker's and shopping excursions in El Paso and Juarez. Finally the trunks were packed with beautiful clothes, for both the Clardy women loved finery, and on a lovely day in early fall, Josephine boarded the train for San Francisco. A sign on the Southern Pacific depot read "To San Francisco, 1285 miles. To New Orleans, 1208 miles."

Josephine was leaving a frontier village where there were no paved streets and no sidewalks. Her long skirts swept the dust when she walked anywhere in El Paso. Consequently she and her mother rented a hack or boarded the mule-drawn streetcar when they went shopping. She hoped San Francisco would be like St. Louis, the sophisticated city where she had lived the previous winter while in boarding school.

Allie Clardy's heart sank as the train pulled out and she started back to her home at 700 Mesa; the big house would seem so empty with

2 A young lieutenant in the Phillipines with the Sixth, who seems to have been a special beau of Josephine.

Josephine on yacht in
San Francisco bay.

Joe-Joe gone. She wondered how she had ever had the courage to send her away. But being a woman of unusual strength, she faced the difficult days ahead with fortitude and determination.

She knew a warm welcome awaited Josephine at the end of her long, tiring train trip. And sure enough, there on the platform in San Francisco when she arrived were Mrs. Loughborough and Marie, who was about Josephine's age, her brothers and several of their young friends. Thus began one of the happiest years in Josephine's life.

The Loughboroughs had been very pleased that Josephine was coming to Berkeley and had sent assurances of welcome. They had a big house and would make a place for her in it. Mary Loughborough's parents lived in Berkeley; her sister and husband were in San Francisco, where the family had many friends. Soon after her arrival, Josephine was enrolled in a fine music school in Berkeley. Mrs. Clardy wrote her on Sept. 21:

I am so pleased to learn that at last you are located [in school] and at work. For I know that when at work your greatest happiness is realized. I do hope that your man teacher will prove a success. . . . I have been very sick, with an infected tooth. Tomorrow Dr. Brady will take it out. . . . Tell me all about your teacher, his method, style, etc. . . . Now goodnight. God bless and keep my darling.

Later she wrote to Joe-Joe that she wanted to devote the year to getting the business affairs straightened out and that afterward the two of them would go somewhere together for a year. She found herself with a great deal of property and knew she would have to learn to manage it. Zeno Clardy's obituary notice had said that he was one of the largest property owners in El Paso. Important people in town were his friends and many of them rallied around now to help Allie get matters in hand. Most helpful of these was Judge W. W. Turney, an able and honest attorney who gave her invaluable advice and assistance. She wrote Josephine:

I do not know what would have become of us if I had not fallen into the hands of Judge Turney . . . he has been very fine and honorable to our interests. Mr. Landry called to say goodbye Sunday morning and I invited him to stay for dinner. He left for New Orleans Monday. He said to tell you he felt deeply hurt at your silence and had hoped against hope that you would some day write to him. Dr. Brady called to see me Tuesday eve — he was surprised that you failed to get his letter.

The young dentist, separated from his wife, must have been lonely and unhappy during this time. Mrs. Clardy later told Josephine that his divorce had been granted. Dr. Brady and Mr. Landry had written Josephine, each saying he had been at the station to tell her goodbye when she left for California; but both had missed her.

In October, Allie wrote that she had received a veil and gloves from Josephine (shopping was much better in San Francisco than in El Paso) and asked if she could get a small hat for her. She also wrote:

I received a dear sweet letter from Lydia this week. Do write her and also Dr. Brady. . . . Mr. Hammett thinks he can make a $54,000 sale for us this week & if so we are alright. Sale of 500 acres of valley land. I do hope it will go through, if so I can go where I wish. Yes, dear, I have been sorely vexed and my life worried out of me, but Mr. Turney is home now and everything is in a fair way to be straightened out again. . . . I don't want you to feel cramped in money matters. Mr. Stevens is in full charge of the rents and has made a good showing for September. Please give me some idea how much your running expenses are and you shall be reinforced. Did you get a new teacher? Write me fully. God bless and keep my little one.

At Thanksgiving, Mrs. Clardy went to St. Louis to visit her sister Lydia and discuss business with Lydia's wealthy husband, Firmin Desloge, who had been a partner with Zeno in purchasing El Paso property. After a few days there, she went on to Walker, Missouri, to visit her parents, Col. and Mrs. Joseph Davis, her father being ill. She wrote Josephine that "everybody in St. Louis was too dear and sweet to me, including Lydia. Please write and thank them for their kindness to me. Firmin Jr. wrote that he could not read your address, so Lydia sent it to him." Josephine's almost illegible handwriting was to plague family and friends for her entire life.

On Thanksgiving Day, Allie wrote a short letter saying she would leave for El Paso the next day. "Grandfather is better and Grandmother has given me some very pretty things. Aunt Emma [Allie's sister] and Mr. Radford are here today. I wish I could see my darling, too. Write to Little Mama in El Paso next letter."

In December Allie wrote Josephine that she hated to disappoint her, but she just could not get away to California for Christmas. She had mailed a box of gifts and "the ring is one dear Papa wanted you to have. Should you not like the glasses, I have arranged to exchange them. I sent Mother Loughborough a beautiful pocketbook. Of course, I knew you would give gifts to Marie, William and Robert, so left it all to you. Little Mama's heart was all for Joe-Joe."

In January she wrote to thank Josephine for her gifts and said she and Clara Hague both felt badly because Josephine thought they had neglected her. On February 20, 1902, she wrote that she was sending Josephine $100. "Clara Hague left last Sat. for New York. She goes to spend a year with Kate. She was so glad to get away from El Paso. Mrs. Hague spent Monday afternoon with me. She sends her best love and wants you to be sure to keep up your correspondence with Clara."

It was a gay winter in Berkeley for Josephine with concerts, operas, her music studies and social activities filling her days. Dashing young Army officers came and went and the beautiful young girl from El Paso had many admirers among them.

Early in May, Josephine returned home. Perhaps she was just homesick, or her mother was ill and lonely. A letter from Marie Loughborough dated May 15 said, "We did feel woe-begone when that train pulled out [for Texas]." She then gave Josephine news of all the recent visitors and of the Loughborough family: "Fannie and Mrs. Mills sent us all — Josephine included — invitations to the commencement exercises at Mills (College). Yesterday the University [of California] had their Class Day exercises. The play was in the big amphitheatre and there were ten thousand people there."

The letter also gave news of the ships plying between 'Frisco and Manila. A friend, Ella McClure, was to sail on the *Thomas* and she did not know a soul on board. "She had a chaperon, who is unable to go, but Mother is going to introduce her to the Captain. Imagine going alone! The *Warren* has put back to Manila with another case of cholera on board. It has been in quarantine ten days and will be for five or ten more. Poor Captain Willie."

A little later Josephine received a letter from her "ever-loving other Mother," Mrs. L. She spoke of Josephine's music and asked, "What did you sing for your mother and how did she like your improvement?" She said Marie had forwarded two letters from Wallie to Josephine and asked how the dear old boy was. She had heard from Major L., who told her to pack up and be ready to move, for his outfit had received orders for home and he thought they would start about the middle of May. She said, "We miss the little girlie who got so tired of us — and hope she will induce her mother to come with her next time. Try to eat and sleep or Wallie won't love you when he comes." There are also references to that other beau named Dick.

In June, Mrs. L. wrote Josephine again, saying they were almost packed and were expecting the Major, along with the whole regiment, to arrive soon, for they have sailed on the *Sherman*. Then there was news of Josephine's teachers at the studio, Mr. Dutton and Mr. Haight, who have been up in Yosemite Valley camping. Miss Wood and her sister have been down at Monterey, but they are gathering at the studio again. However, it was to be closed during July. "He [your teacher] is afraid you will not keep up your work while at home. And says you must be sure to come back this fall to prepare for next winter. Mr. Furness is to give big things, whole scenes in costume. I really do not see much chance of visiting you just now as everybody thinks the regiment will go the other way. . . . How exciting your fire was — you could have had quite a romantic rescue in Dr. B's arms."

It was true, the regiment went the other way, arriving for station at Fort Leavenworth, Kansas. In July, Major Loughborough himself wrote Josephine from that post saying how much he regretted not seeing her when he arrived in San Francisco. "Had I had the routing of the regiment from Frisco here, I assure you that El Paso would have been on the way." In fact, he would have preferred to be stationed there again, he said.

"We had a cold trip most of the way from Nagasaki," he wrote, "and the sun was visible but once after leaving there. We were two days in Japan and a party of us took rickashaws [sic] and went over the mountain to Moji; the scenery is grand and you see some beautiful sights. The climate is the most salubrious in the world . . . but should I never see our far off possessions again, am sure I will survive it." He asked Josephine to come to visit them and mentioned the fact that there were about a hundred officers on post and ninety-seven more expected soon. A visit there must have sounded very interesting to Josephine but no record that she went has been found.

Her good friend, Clara Hague, however, who was visiting her sister Kate and her Army officer husband at another post, was having the time of her life. The Laubachs were at Plattsburg, N.Y., and Clara wrote Josephine from there in July, 1902, saying:

The post is so terribly gay that we haven't a minute to call our own. Instead of getting fat and taking care of myself, I spend all my time with the rest of the garrison, taking in everything that is going on. But I'm going to have all the fun I can, for I've never had it before and surely never expect to in El Paso. Last night Kate gave a card party and had all the young people on the post and a few of the married ones. The post is full of visiting girls . . . there is a sweet girl from Nashville, who plays piano beautifully so I've lost my mind about her just on that account.

Last Friday night, the whole post went up to the Champlain Hotel to dinner. We had a fine time, after dinner they had fireworks and then we danced until twelve. I have already told you what a beautiful place it is. It is filled with millionaires but I think the Army people have the best time for they do all the dancing and the guests sit back and look on. I hope to go up several times before the season is over, for the hotel keeps open only two months.

My dear I would love to hear you sing. I know you have gotten over your nervousness or you would not be singing in the church. I am glad you have met the nice men at Bliss. I hope there will be a few left when I get home. Margaret C. is engaged to an Army officer. She is the beauty that has been with Lill since Feb. She has had the most beautiful time. All the men have simply lost their minds about her. Oh! my dear, how lovely it is to be beautiful.

In the spring of 1904 Mrs. Loughborough wrote to Josephine from Ft. Leavenworth telling her of Marie's wedding. She was distressed because her recent letters to Josephine, sent to New York and El Paso, had not been answered. In fact, Josie's invitation to Marie's wedding came back from the dead letter office, she said, but she knew that Mrs. Clardy received her invitation because wedding gifts had come from her.

"Marie looked lovely in a white silk gown, carrying a shower bouquet of bride's roses; the six bridesmaids were dressed alike in white silk tissue with ruffled skirts and having blue silk tissue scarfs around their shoulders." Mrs. L.'s father officiated and the groomsmen, nearly all from the Sixth Regiment, were in full dress uniforms. She described the wedding:

Such a jam as the house was at the reception! It's a big house but there were at least three hundred people. Her presents were exquisite and such loads of them. Among those she prizes most were the lovely forks you sent. She had nothing like them. There were several cut glass bowls and a silver one, also chocolate sets. Very few of her things were duplicates, only about 17 bon bon dishes of silver and a dozen cut glass ones. Several larger cut glass bowls, several lettuce forks and several dozen tea spoons.

Mrs. L. spoke of a recent visit of a young friend of Josephine's from El Paso, Anne Kemp [later Mrs. Hugh White]. "Anne Kemp used to say to me, now Mrs. L. today you better write to Josephine Clardy for even if you have not heard from her, you know she is away from home, sick and having trouble with her eyes." Mrs. L. concluded by saying "Now dear, if you get this please send me some word for I have been much bothered about you."

During one of the winters Josephine spent in New York (probably 1902 or 1903), she studied voice with Emilio Agramonte, who wrote her a letter after she had returned home in the spring, saying how much he missed her when the clock pointed to 11:45 a.m., the hour for her lesson. He wrote, part in English and part in French: At this hour "it seems to me that you have to appear a few minutes later. Alas! your bright face and sweet smile are missing, just the memory remains. . . . How is your voice? Your confidence? When you come back I shall make you sing duetts [sic] and trios and quartettes and shall make you sing before people, organizing small gatherings among my pupils, so that you may completely lose that fear and acquire aplomb and confidence about your singing."

Agramonte said he had a proposition to make Josephine. "Last year

I received from you in tuition fees from the 5th of September to April 15 $320 — my offer is for half of the amount, $160 to give you lessons for the same period if you can advance me the money now, that I need it very much before going to Louisiana. . . . I shall give you lessons every day like this year and take the same interest I took."

About this same time, Josephine took part in a public musical in El Paso which was called a "Lullaby Concert," held in the First Presbyterian Church. She sang two solos, "Last Night" by Kjerulf and "Cradle Song" by Vannah. Among the dozen or so musicians appearing on the program was Mrs. W. D. Howe, who had been soloist at the funeral of Josephine's father. The music critic commented in the newspaper account that most of those participating "are well known favorites with the music lovers of El Paso and need no commendation from the press. But Miss Clardy is a new star and sang her way to the hearts of the audience last night. She possesses a sweet, well trained and sympathetic voice."

Very little else is recorded about Josephine as a music student but it seems certain that she studied quite seriously for a number of years. The scant records include a receipted bill from Kate Moore in El Paso, paid by Mrs. Clardy for her daughter's piano lessons. There is also evidence that from time to time she studied music with an El Paso voice teacher, Mrs. Stockwell.

One of her teachers was Orrie Mae Coons of Los Angeles, who had been a pupil of Edward MacDowell. In Sept. 1907 Mrs. Coons wrote Miss Clardy, who was then in Los Angeles: "How are you getting on with your music? I am at home again after a pleasant outing, but I shall not give any lessons before the first of next month. However, I am making all arrangements for my winter class, and should like to hear from you as to your plans. If you wish to continue your study with me, kindly let me know so I can save the time for you. Did you know that Signor is coming back? I know you are happy to hear that. Let me hear from you as soon as possible for I shall be very busy this winter and am getting everything arranged now."

In later years, Josephine must have given up her own music entirely, for nobody seems to have heard of her sitting down to the piano to play or sing even the simplest melodies. In fact, the piano which she had in her home at 1119 Montana was a Steinway player, and it was in a very sad state of repair when she died. It was sold after Pearson Wosika repaired it.

Occasionally, she did recall the days when she sang in public. Once in later life, when she was seated beside a friend[3] at a luncheon, opera houses were being discussed and she remarked that she had sung in every major opera house in Europe, except La Scala. This was an obvious fantasy, perhaps reflecting a youthful ambition.

[3] Interview, Mrs. Howard Quinn, January, 1973.

CHARLES G. McGHEE
*Important in the life of Josephine
during the next few years.*

CHAPTER IV

Interlude with Charley

⋦§ ALTHOUGH HER TEACHERS HAD WANTED Josephine to return to Berkeley in the fall of 1902 to continue studying music, she decided instead to go to New York. The El Paso *Herald* reported in December, 1902: "Mrs. Z. B. Clardy has returned from New York City where she had been visiting her daughter, Miss Josephine Clardy, who is studying music in New York under a noted musician."

Miss Clardy arrived in New York at the age of 21. Possessed of remarkable beauty and charm, she soon made friends and found herself in a new and exciting world. She was to return year after year to this world where opera, the theatre, fine restaurants and luxurious hotels beckoned her to a life she loved.

One of the friends she met that first winter in the city was to have a great influence on her life for the next few years. His name was Charles G. McGhee, a widower several years older than Josephine, and a man of considerable education and culture. A member of the New York Cotton Exchange, he was associated with the brokerage firm of Daniel O'Dell & Co. Josephine preserved many of his letters, all of which he signed simply "Charley." They give an insight into that period of her life.

Charley fell deeply in love with Josephine and wished to marry her. She enjoyed his company and basked in the warmth of his love and admiration. For a time she appeared to have agreed to an engagement and the relationship went on for several years. Unfortunately Charley's health was not good and he had to work too hard. He spoke of his debts and an obligation that was like "a millstone" about his neck. Perhaps he had obligated himself heavily to buy into the firm. At one time he wrote Joe that he was on the verge of a breakdown and needed a rest, saying that his mother had offered to lend him the money "to square things here but I wouldn't take it." Charley's mother, who owned a plantation in Mississippi, came to New York for several months during the social season.

Some time early in her friendship with Charley, Josephine sustained the eye injury that eventually led to the partial loss of sight. She was treated in New York over a period of years by an eminent eye physician, Dr. Weeks. In a letter dated Jan. 5, 1905 Charley wrote Josephine, "I rode up on the car with Weeks yesterday and he asked after you and particularly about your mother. He says you will surely be able to read big print with your injured eye and the spot will practically disappear."

Josephine's grandmother, Mrs. Rebecca Davis, who had been visiting her daughter Mollie in Poston, New Mexico, came to El Paso to spend Christmas of 1904 with Allie and Joe, staying for a few weeks. She was not well and found it hard to be content anywhere away from her old home and friends in Missouri, but Colonel Davis had died some two years earlier and their home had been broken up.

Aunt Mollie had written Josephine that fall, begging her to write her grandmother as often as possible, "for she is so sad and lonely here." Writing about Joe's eye trouble, Aunt Mollie said: "I can't tell you how thankful I am to know that you can even distinguish light with your eye. I have prayed so earnestly that you might have its sight restored. Don't get discouraged. I was practically blind in my right eye for years. Now that eye is as good as the other almost, though not quite so strong. Don't relax your efforts to improve your eye."

Charley McGhee wrote in January from New York: "I am awfully sorry your Grandma is ill and hope the mild climate of El Paso will soon build her up again." Then slipping into the language of love, he wrote, "It's an awfully comfortable feeling to be married [promised?] again. The bachelors may brag as much as they please, but I'm satisfied! But it's like being married by proxy. You are so far away and kisses have time to get cold and lonesome when confided to the tender mercies of Uncle Sam's mail bags for almost 4 days."

On December 13, 1906 Charley wrote Josephine: "Well I've plugged away until I can plug no longer and have cut it all now and am going home for a month or two. The doctors can't find anything wrong. I have just gotten tired and lost all the flesh I ever had. You know I haven't had a day's vacation since I joined the Exchange . . .

and nothing but sickness has kept me away. But don't bother about it as I really have nothing the matter and I think the air and rest will put me in better shape than ever."

Charley did get away from New York; he went with his mother to Columbus, Mississippi, where he hoped to get out in the fields with his gun and dog. He wrote that he wondered if the "throb, throb of Broadway will keep up in my ears?" even in the country.

Josephine and her mother were in Los Angeles at Hampden Arms at that time. She wrote Charley in Mississippi asking if he had taken her two pictures along. He replied: "You know I have 5 pictures not 2 of you, that including the one taken when you were a baby. The picture I referred to is one I left at home because Sue and Mama asked me, but the one in a frame once used for Modjeska has always been with me. It is the one taken when you were a school girl and is a profile. It does not look very like you now but is very much to my fancy."

He continued: "I am distressed that you are still suffering with your eyes. You owe it to yourself to give music up for a long time if not forever. Modjeska[1] said a thing to me once that I have never forgotten. I had heard of the wonderful singing voice that she had as a girl and asked her once after she had played some little thing why she had never kept her music up. She said that as soon as she realized she could not give it all the time it deserved, she determined to devote the rest of her life to enjoying it (music) and let other people do the work."

By 1907 relations were not going so smoothly between Josephine and Charley. A man whom she had met in El Paso some four years earlier was looming large in the picture and, through persistent courtship, was winning his way into her heart. This man was Eugene Fox, who would finally become her husband.

But Charley had not given up hope and on May 16, 1907 he wrote to Josephine, who was again in Los Angeles: "I met some friends of yours Sunday at Mrs. DuBose', Mr. and Mrs. Coles. Of course we spoke of you and I felt like writing to you. . . . Coles understands you I think and certainly admires you. I was surprised to hear him speak of you just as I would in regard to your ideas and sense of duty and

[1] Helena Modjeska (1840-1909), the Polish-born actress, later one of the most famous American dramatic actresses of her era.

obligation. It was very pleasant to me to talk about you. It was almost like seeing you and from what they say I may see you in the fall. I wish you could write me more about things. But I don't suppose you ever will now. Well I'm waiting for a letter. Devotedly, Charley."

When Josephine wrote him later that month giving him the *coup de grace* in farewell, she must have indicated that she planned to marry Mr. Fox, even though she did not enter into a formal engagement until after she and her mother had spent a year in Europe. Poor Charley accepted the sentence gracefully, although he told her she was still his ideal woman and that he loved her past all understanding and would always do so. He did want to see her again, he said, before she left for that long trip "on a road that leads forever the other way."

If they met again, no record exists of their encounter.

In her love affair with Charley, Josephine may have first realized her power to evoke strong emotions in a man, feelings that could not be turned on and off at will by such a man as he. In one of his letters Charley told her that he had taught her the meaning of love; he had taught her how to love. "When I said that I taught you to love, I referred entirely to whatever of passion your heart knows. It was a testament to the pure white of your soul." And again, he wrote: "You know, sweetheart, nobody in the world ever had one tenth your power to make love when you want to. I'd give the world (now) for just one kiss."

Although his own passions had been intense and fierce, he realized that Josephine no longer cared for him as she once had; she had changed and so had he. He wrote that he never felt the same toward her after he became convinced that she could let him suffer in comparative indifference. "It seemed as if I burned my heart out in the fierce jealousy and long anxious waiting to hear from you. But dearest Josephine, this is not a reproach, only an attempt to make it easy for you to tell me what I am sure it is now time for you to tell."

Later, Eugene Fox was to experience this same seeming heartless treatment from Josephine before she finally capitulated and married him. No doubt his feelings were equally intense, but he was not as articulate as was Charley McGhee.

CHAPTER V

Innocents Abroad

∽§ EVER SINCE 1901 when Myra Newman had gone to Germany with the Austins of El Paso, Josephine had wanted to go to Europe. Myra had written glowing letters about the operas, concerts and plays she was enjoying. She longed for Josephine to come over and share these great experiences with her. Allie had wanted to take Joe-Joe to Europe to spend a year, but she had to wait until the business affairs were in good shape. So Josephine went to California that winter of 1901 and then to New York for study and fun, while Allie stayed close to El Paso, building a safe financial base for them both.

Now it was June, 1908, and the two women were finally about to embark on the great adventure. Josephine had broken off her engagement to Charley McGhee and had agreed to an informal arrangement with Eugene Fox — they were engaged to be engaged, as it were, the wedding plans to be made following her year abroad.

At the last moment, Eugene announced he was going along! He had arranged for a month's vacation from his office with the EP & SW and would accompany them. How nice it was to have a man along to handle all the details of travel; how reassuring for two women venturing into a strange world, not to arrive there alone. Eugene was a tall, broad-shouldered, handsome man, whose friendly smile and ready wit made friends for him quickly wherever he went. He adored both Josephine and her mother, and Allie trusted him implicitly.

It seemed for a while that they might have a fourth person along. Josephine had a dear little dressmaker named Bessie Promontorio, who was also her landlady in New York and her friend. When Bessie had received Josephine's letter (half of which she declared she was unable to read) telling of the proposed trip to Europe, she replied at once, proposing that she would like to join them, for she and her husband, Ernest, were planning to spend three months in Italy. They expected to leave New York in July, but if she could travel with the

Clardys, she would go in June as she would love to show Joe-Joe the sights of Paris. Ernest could join them later. "And for God's sake, Josephine, when you reply, let your mother be the scribe, or use the typewriter!" she begged. Since the Clardys and Mr. Fox had already engaged their passage, the plan did not work out. But they did see Bessie and Ernest in Italy.

The Promontorios were newlyweds and Bessie told Josephine that she had just found out that Ernest was a Marquis, the title having come down through his father's family for five centuries. The family had come from Geneva, where a street was named for them. Ernest had been reluctant to tell her all this, she said, because "they are now poor." However, Ernest had a brother in Naples, who was a prosperous diamond merchant, and he was to visit them in New York in September. "This title business is a secret for a while," Bessie said, "as I don't care to be laughed at about it, although it is no joke."

After disembarking at Liverpool, the El Pasoans went to London and there met and spent a few days with their dear friends, Lettie Emerson and her daughters, Babe and Helen, the girls being near Josephine's age. They had been in Europe for several months and were now returning to the States, but not to El Paso directly. They would go to Montreal, thence to their own summer island home on Rose Island at the mouth of the St. Lawrence River. Helen and Ed McIntyre were to be married there in late August. Ed's mother and sister had joined the Emersons in Europe and toured with them for a month or so before they met the Clardys in London.

From Florence, Italy, where she had taken an apartment, Lettie Emerson had written Allie Clardy a long letter in March, relating some of their experiences and outlining plans which served, perhaps, as a guide for the Clardys when they followed along the same route. She wrote:

We have had a grand time here. . . . When we saw the Pope, we had the same audience with Prince Charles of Bourbon and his newly converted English bride. We spent three-quarters of an hour in the Grand Salon with them. Here in Florence we go out to the lovely villas, etc. and it is a city of homes, palaces, etc. Babe has a crowd of college girls (Vassar, Smith, etc.) and some young English and Irish men in the drawing room. They had planned a picnic in the country, but it is raining and so had to have it here. This is where "Romolo" lived — she was a Bardi. On our hall entrance is an alabaster lion by Donatello. The marble mantel is one from the 11th Century — I am having it copied. Are you really coming over? We will meet you at the Ritz London. I wish you could have been here with us. We go to musicals, operas, etc. all invites. When you are here, I will give you a note to a vocal chap, Braggioto — he is rich and they have a gorgeous villa with concert hall, etc. Babe takes [lessons] from Maestro Pavesi-Bassi's teacher.

We have some glad rags — found I could buy the Paris models here so cheap. Will get hats in Paris, a lace coat for myself, a travelling suit for Helen in Vienna. We have all else — dandy linen embroidery and Italian inlet work — and parasols. So I shan't buy a scrap for two years. Do travel slowly — So silly to rush. I could tell you some of the things we have seen — but you must see it all. We have enjoyed Florence, its culture, clean streets, all of marble. And flowers — my, I wish we had flowers in El Paso. They grow wild here everywhere.

From Florence she said they would go to Venice, Budapest, Vienna, Dresden, Berlin, then down the Rhine to Cologne, on to Holland, Brussels, Paris, England, Ireland and Scotland, then back to London to meet the Clardys. Quite a tour.

And now Joe, her mother and Eugene covered much of this same territory before Eugene had to leave them. The Clardys went to Paris to spend the winter, renting a small villa there. Josephine studied vocal music and practised French with a tutor, having already acquired some command of the language during school days in St. Louis.

Scant recorded information remains about the winter in Europe, except that Miss Josephine Clardy made some conquests, as she seemed to do wherever she went in those youthful days, and these attentive young men showed her the town in both Paris and London. The winter was cold and rainy in Paris and the weather was foul when they went to London in the spring. Allie Clardy, whose health was frail, was sick often and Josephine had occasional colds and slight illnesses. They consulted eye specialists who were not able to do much for poor Josephine. She told someone years later that one European doctor put the wrong poultices on her eye and made the condition worse.

Although their daily activities can not be traced in detail during that winter, we know that Allie and Josephine saw the famous sights, attended the important musical events, went to the races and, above all, achieved two much-sought-after honors, an audience with the Pope and a presentation at the Court of St. James. For years, Josephine kept the gloves and fan, along with the royal invitations, in a little box, which she showed to friends. Her presentation gown and Allie's must have been lovely indeed. As they both loved clothes, they sought and found the best dressmakers on the continent, for they brought home loads of beautiful clothes, hats, laces, French lingerie and other finery.

When the summer of 1909 arrived and it was time for the Clardys to return home, Josephine cabled Eugene from the Savoy Hotel, where they had been staying in London, advising him of their sailing date and asking if he would meet them in New York. Eugene's headquarters at that time was Chicago, but he had been spending a week at the Brown Palace in Denver when he received Josephine's cable. He had written her from there that it was a relief to get away from the summer heat of Chicago, but that of all things, he was just recovering from whooping cough. "Did you ever hear of such a ridiculous thing? A full grown man to have such juvenile ailments!"

He would be delighted to meet Joe and Allie in New York, he cabled them. It had been a long, lonely year for Eugene, separated by so many miles from his beloved.

When they arrived in New York, Allie stayed only long enough to get Josephine settled in the Waldorf Hotel, then she hurried home, for Eugene had brought news that several properties, including some of her stores, had burned down on Broadway (now South Mesa) Street in El Paso. Josephine was staying in New York to go back to Dr. Weeks for treatment of her eyes.

In London, an Englishman, Henry C. N. Harding, a playwright and poet, had fallen in love with Josephine and his letters followed her to New York. In small, tightly formed letters, unbelievably illegible, he wrote beautiful prose. Josephine's hand was a large, loose script, equally unreadable, which causes us to wonder if either could make out what the other was writing.

Henry had introduced the Texas girl to his friends in London, many of whom belonged to the nobility. He said he hoped she would like his friends, for he was sure he was going to win her hand and bring her to London to live. He had already won her heart, he said. He had taken her to the opera and they had heard Tetrazzini sing, who was, he thought, in good voice. Before she left London, she had received a note from him saying:

Lady Margaret is looking forward to meeting you tomorrow at tea at 4:30 at the Carlton and after that I am going to have my talk with your mother. I'd like to wring that little Count's neck for daring to propose to you, he's barely known you a week. He'd not have dared to do so if you'd had a brother or father about. I hope on Friday to take you over to the Royal Stables. Hope some flowers arrived for you yesterday! What a ripping frock you wore last night & the most fascinating twisty thing in your hair. Eh bien.

Henry remembered that it was just a few days before she sailed that "I blurted out that I wanted to marry you. I wonder if you'll think of it? I don't believe anyone was ever in a worse fright than I was then. I knew just what I wanted to say, but of course couldn't say it." He wanted Josephine to understand how shy Englishmen are and said they are not cold and reserved, as she might think, but just terribly shy. Later he wrote her:

I wonder if it interests you to know that the Scottish Repertoire Theater manager has practically decided to do my play, but I don't consider this fixed until everything is signed and sealed. Also I hear from a third person who knows him that he thinks the one act of my blank verse play that I sent him . . . the finest he has ever seen. Why don't you write me a little line? I know at the bottom of my heart that we were made for each other . . . even if you should write me that you are engaged, it would not discourage me. I know that in your heart you love me and I would just wait a while longer.

The Count that Henry spoke of must have been the Frenchman, Yvon de la Motte, member of a prominent family in France. They had met in Paris just before Josephine and her mother had gone on to London. He wrote her at the Savoy saying he hoped she had received his "long bad English letter written Saturday." He had been to London to see her and then after returning to Paris, found himself very miserable, with "no taste to see anybody." He had been for a long walk in *le bois*, "thinking on you and your mother, liking [wishing] to go there." He had met friends of Josephine, a New York banker and his wife named Mr. and Mrs. Learing. He wrote:

Tonight I will write to Mr. Learing in New York and ask him what he has to give about his business and if he wants to come back here soon —

and also I will ask him to take me over to America and give me a chance to be in his bank or in any business there. It would be to me so agreeable to go there and to prove to you that outside of horses, country life, or theatre and Boulevard, I am able to do something useful. Because I think you must have a very poor idea of my sentiment of the life and I would like so much that you might consider me better than you thought. I miss you very much.

Specially in the evening, we had such a lovely time we three together. I recognize that you did tease me a great deal but if I did myself the same, it might have been to give you back what you made to me.

He said he was going to imagine what she would be doing that evening (she was to go to Covent Garden to the opera) — how her hair would be "placed" (arranged), the color of her gown and so on. "Only one thing I will not be able to discover, perhaps, your look. Notwithstanding, I hope your smile will appear but do not give it to the Englishman."

Some weeks later he was in a small lakeside resort in Switzerland, writing to Josephine at the Astor Hotel in New York. She had written him aboard ship, then again from New York, making him very happy. He said, "I thank you very much for having not forgot to tell me about you. You tell me you are going to spend the weekend with the Learings, where? Was it in the Catskill Mountains or in the New Jersey Coast? . . . I think that instead of being in New York you would have been much better here taking a cure of delightful air, drinking milk and eating the good Swiss food."

He speaks again of the hope that he might go to New York and work for Mr. Learing, this time on the Delaware and Eastern Railway. In closing he sent kind regards to her mother and "all my best thoughts to you. I do kiss your hand, Yvon de la Motte."

During the winter that Josephine and her mother were in France, she and Clara Hague, though oceans apart, were keeping in touch by letter. Josephine had written Clara about the attentions of the Count and seemed to indicate considerable interest in the gentleman. Clara's reply was written aboard the Transport Buford in the harbor at Guam as she, her sister Kate and husband, Capt. H. L. Laubach, were steaming toward his station in the Philippines. Clara and Kate were in mourning for their mother, who had just died in El Paso, and they were stricken because they had not been with her at the last. Clara wrote:

The boat is full to the top and lots of interesting, fascinating officers, but with our great sorrow so fresh, it's hard to be agreeable to anyone. One of Mr. Dodge's best friends is on board and a perfect dear. His name is Roderick Dear and it quite suits him. He has been lovely to me and am so glad he is to be at our station.

I think often of the dear Count, and hope dear by this time you have completely won him. Do tell me all the news. Letters from home will be so good to get. Can hardly wait for news. Remember me to the Count. Don't forget. Lots of love to your mother and dear self.

Josephine preserved the Count's letters, some of which he wrote in French. It would seem that Mr. Learing did not feel the need of the services of a French "man of the boulevard" and so poor Count Yvon la Motte must never have reached the United States.

Chapter VI

Home Again

 When Allie got back to El Paso, she found business almost at a standstill and the August heat almost unbearable. She wrote Joe that she had gone into an apartment at 1510 N. El Paso St. and said she hoped to rent the home at 700 Mesa (which had apparently been leased during her year's absence). Ted Cooley, who sometimes helped in her business, was out of town, but Grover Smith was on the job looking after her properties for the firm of J. H. Smith and Sons.

None of her buildings on Broadway had burned down, but they were damaged and she would lose some rent. Also the "valley was not cut off, just overflowed on a part next to Val Verde," as it had done before. She said that "things look very gloomy just now and I really am uneasy about the next few years, but I will hope for the best. Take good care of your precious self and don't worry about mama." She said that Eugene had come by to see her every night, but she had not been anywhere as it had been "too hot to go out of the house."

She said that Myra Newman (who had married C. J. Mapel and now had a darling little daughter, Fanny) had been by to see her several times and was anxious to hear about the trip. She had invited Allie over to spend the day with her, but Mrs. Clardy could not go because she was fixing up the house and had painters working.

About this time Josephine received a long letter from Myra, who enclosed a picture of little Fanny (later Mrs. Porter Thompson). Myra spoke of how disappointed she was that Josephine had not come back to El Paso with her mother. "I am sure I am not the only one who was disappointed. You know I have a very warm spot in my heart for Mr. Fox and he is such a splendid fellow that I had hoped he would persuade you to come home, Josephine. You have many friends who are anxious to see you and I don't think you would find El Paso so bad, although I know it is far from Paris or New York. But after all there is much more in life than just the superficial pleasures. But this really wasn't meant for a sermon, so enough."

Myra then gave news of mutual El Paso friends: "The Nations wedding [Katherine Nations to Studebaker Riley] will be 'pulled off' in a few days. I suppose Katherine has some beautiful clothes but I am crazy to see yours. I know they must be lovely and you a picture in them. Josie [the former Josephine Magoffin] is home this winter as Captain Glasgow is in the Phillipines. You have probably heard that Edith [Newman, a cousin] married Rob Reynolds last Thursday in Los Angeles . . . we are all so happy that Edith is happily married. . . . Write soon and above all come home soon as I will be lost without either you or Edith this winter. Loads of love, Myra."

When Eugene had to make a quick trip to California, he asked Allie if she would not like to go along and escape from the El Paso heat for a few days. She did so and it must have helped her spirits as well as her physical well being.

She wrote Joe: "Eugene and I had a glorious trip and had you only been with us, it would have been perfect. Eugene was just as dear & sweet to me as he could be. He is awfully blue & I have told him if he would only be patient for a short time you would come home and then get married. I have done all I could but sometimes he simply refuses to be put off any longer & he certainly has been good. I want you to write me fully about your eye and nose as I feel very uneasy about you. I want you to stay as long as the Dr. thinks it necessary & then come home."

Later, Allie went to a wedding reception and wrote Josephine that everyone was simply lovely to her. "Mrs. Charles Newman was the first to come up and speak to me; Ethel White and Miss White, everybody came up and spoke & so glad to welcome me home. Mrs. Turney was simply all smiles & talked with me quite a while; complimented my good looks and 'fine' dress. Also Mrs. Rose, Mrs. Berrien and Mrs. Will Race. It would have made you very happy to have seen your little momma so much made over. In my heart I know it was my beautiful gown. I was very glad to go and wore one of my best gowns — my yellow. Everybody simply raved over how well I looked & how beautiful my dress was."

By November, Allie was planning to borrow the money to improve the Broadway property (that is, build something on it) as she said "it is too valuable to let it stay idle any longer." She expected to go to St. Louis to confer with Mr. Desloge about it, as she would have to improve some of the Desloge & Clardy property to pay the taxes. She was evidently a shrewd business woman, for she said:

We will make money by holding everything but will have to put up better houses to hold and pay taxes. I have really been too busy to see anyone. Myra is coming in tomorrow but the house is still unfinished but will be this week. Mrs. Foster & Emory came & spent Sunday afternoon with me. Mrs. Turner spent yesterday forenoon. Everybody is busy going to the Horse Show & fair. I have not been able to go as I have had to go every day until today to the cemetery. Your father's monument is perfectly beautiful — it is all finished and paid for & I am certainly very proud of it. Everybody thinks it the handsomest thing in the State of Texas. I know you will be pleased. Now precious one write & tell me all about yourself & what you are going to do & let me know about your eye and nose. I am well but awfully lonesome at times, but it will soon be all right & we will be happy when we can be together again. Write to Eugene at once.

Eugene is still unsettled & I feel very sorry for him. It will break my heart if he leaves El Paso. Please write me how your eye is getting along & how long you think it necessary to remain in NY. I do not want you to come home until Dr. Weeks tells you he has done everything in his power for you & pray that he is doing you good. While I sometimes feel that I cannot do without you one other day — I do not allow myself to act selfishly when your dear little eyes are to suffer thereby.

I have written Bess twice since I came [home] from Calif. but have not had an ans. Please tell her that it is too late for me to think of getting any dress this winter. I don't see how you can do without a good street tailor made & I want you to get one before you come home. How did you like your coat. Josie Nations came to see me Friday. I heard when in Los Angelus that Josie & Ramsey Bagy had been having a great flirtation when Josie was out there last summer. She was amazed to know that I had heard about it & that we knew the Bagys. The world is so small after all.

I have just attended Nina Neff's shower given by Mrs. Campbell. Everybody was there & lovely to me. Adell Coles came up and spoke very sweetly to me & apologized for not speaking to me at Kitty Nations wedding. Said she really did not know me I was looking so much better. Please get a photo for Mrs. Pfaff. She is lovely to me. Don't rush home until you are ready to come.

Allie and Josephine were both fond of Bessie Promontorio and it is probable that Allie kept up with Joe-Joe by corresponding with Bessie during the fall and winter of 1909 after their return from Europe. Joe was a poor letter-writer and direct news from her did not come to

Allie as frequently as she would have liked. But her link with Bessie was broken in 1910 when the Promontorios left New York and took up residence in Naples.

It is likely that Bessie did not know Eugene Fox, or if she knew him, did not know that he and Josephine planned to marry. She wrote a delightful letter to Joe from Naples in December, 1910, showing off some of her newly learned Italian by addressing her friend as "my dear Giuseppina." Bessie said she longed for Joe every day and was sure she would be happy in Naples. "It must have been very dull when you were in Naples last July, as the social season does not start until after Christmas and continues until May. People are still in the country. Our Princess (a tenant of ours) is still in the country. We are so centrally, exclusively and delightfully located, can hear music in the park and have a glorious view . . . from the balcony I can look down into beautiful gardens which have orange, lemon and tangerine trees full of fruit; roses and many other flowers are blooming. The long terrace is finished in white Carrara marble and there are large camellia trees in full bloom.

Then she gets to the point of her letter: "Honey, do come and make me a *long visit* — I am now *inviting* you to take pot luck and can only promise to do the best I can to make you comfortable." She says the only expense for Josephine would be her laundry, which they sent out. But best of all — Bessie has picked out a husband for Josephine! He was her husband's brother, Albert. He had a large, splendid apartment on the other side of the building, she said. He was handsome and rich, 38 or 39 years old, dignified, even tempered, and clever. He was getting richer every year, and he belonged to the old nobility. He was moral, high-minded and had all sorts of other virtues. She continued: "If there ever were two people made for each other in this world, you and Albert are the two."

Bessie added: "It is quite nice to be a foreigner for a change. One has much less responsibility. We could have a dandy lot of fun, Josephine. COME ON OVER AS SOON AS EVER YOU CAN AND LET'S BE GAY & HAPPY for as many months as you care to stay, a year if you like or more." Then she remembered about Mrs. Clardy and says she would make room for her also.

But Josephine did not avail herself of this generous offer and so did not marry the Italian paragon, Albert.

CHAPTER VII

Mr. Fox Comes Courting

ৰ্জ WHEN EUGENE FOX CAME TO EL PASO IN 1904, his first friends included men who were to be numbered among the city's most influential business leaders. They were Charles N. Bassett, a wealthy young man about Gene's age and two older fellows, George D. Flory and Maury Edwards. Flory and Edwards were friends and both were employees of Charles' father, O. T. Bassett, who had died January 4, 1898.

Soon after his graduation from college in 1901, Charles Bassett came to El Paso to take charge of his father's extensive business interests. The three men "formed a bachelor triumvirate and set up housekeeping on San Antonio Street, across from the Baptist Church."[1] By the time Gene Fox arrived, the Toltec Club had been built just across the street from the bachelors' upstairs apartment and Gene had a room in the club. He was welcomed into the fraternity of bachelors and they lived a carefree life that many men might envy.

Gene Fox, who was travel and freight agent for the El Paso and Southwestern Railroad, was not as well off as the three others in the group, but he managed to keep up his part fairly well and it made no difference to the others, anyway.

"Stories still circulate about their escapades," C. L. Sonnichsen says. "They bought their whiskey by the gallon and lived according to their desires without apology or concealment. A loyal colored woman Annie Scott Griggs, looked after them and loved them all."[2] Eugene, tall, handsome and good-natured, soon became known as quite a fellow about town and a popular member of the Social Club.

Soon after his arrival in El Paso, Eugene met the beautiful Miss Josephine Clardy — and it was love at first sight as far as he was con-

[1] C. L. Sonnichsen, *The State National Since 1881* (El Paso: Texas Western Press, 1971), p. 65.   [2] Ibid.

cerned. Neither Maury Edwards, manager of the Bassett Lumber Yard, nor George Flory, an officer of the State National Bank, ever married. The first of the bachelors to succumb was Charles Bassett, who married Miss Myra Powers in 1915 and brought her to El Paso to live. A few months later, Eugene and Josephine were married in New York City and went to Chicago to reside as that was then Eugene's headquarters. Although he and Charles Bassett remained friends always, their wives never seemed to have much in common and saw little of each other.

Eugene Fox had come to El Paso from St. Louis, where he was traveling passenger agent for the Rock Island Railroad. His parents were John L. and Sabrina Taylor Fox, who were married in Council Bluffs, Iowa in 1871. They were living in Winterset, Iowa, when Eugene was born in 1877. He had two sisters, Gertrude and Eva, and a brother, Leo. The family moved to Hutchinson, Kansas, in 1892 and later to Kansas City. After receiving his education in public schools, Eugene began his career in railroading in Hutchinson, where he was yard and then freight house bill clerk for the Rock Island.

In 1920 Eugene Fox returned to Hutchinson for a visit, traveling in his private railroad car "Nacozari." The editor of the Hutchinson *Gazette* described his rise in railroad circles as "meteoric," and acclaimed him as one of the city's most prominent sons of whose success "the Salt City is justly proud." At that time Eugene was General Traffic Manager of the EP & SW with offices in El Paso.

Eugene's courtship of Josephine had many ups and downs. He often suffered from loneliness, sometimes from jealousy and often from apparent indifference on her part when they were separated, which was often. He was a prolific letter writer, posting a letter a day to Josephine over long periods of time. She wrote with difficulty and hated the effort involved; consequently her letters were infrequent. Over and over Eugene wrote telling her she was "the dearest, prettiest and best little girl in all the world" and saying he simply could not live without her. He considered himself pledged to her and wrote that he had never paid any attention to any other woman since he first met her.

For years Josephine seemed unable to make up her mind about Eugene. She admired him and undoubtedly was very fond of him; certainly both she and her mother depended on him in a great many ways. But there were other men in the picture, and perhaps Josephine was not ready to settle down with any one of them.

Some women do not reach emotional maturity at an early age, some never. Josephine, an only child, was over-protected by her devoted parents; following her father's untimely death, she became her mother's constant companion. This must have led to an unnatural dependency on her mother, coupled with a sense of duty that made her feel it would be disloyal to marry. Eugene, possessed of a strong paternal, protective instinct, may have contributed to this immaturity without realizing its self-defeating result. During the years of Eugene's courtship, Josephine was spending several months in New York in the winter and living in California in the summer. She and her mother went to the coast to escape the heat, as did many other El Paso women.

Josephine loved New York, the hub of the musical and theatrical world, where there was always activity and gaiety. She had a circle of sophisticated friends and her beauty and wit won her many admirers. Then also she was studying music and she felt that she might one day have a career if she persevered, especially if she could spend a few years with good teachers in Europe, where it was believed the truly fine teachers were to be found.

In 1905 and 1906 Eugene was working for EP & SW out of the Los Angeles office and living in the Jonathan Club there, where a relative, Charles Fox, had a membership. On January 18, 1906, Eugene wrote Josephine in El Paso, saying, "This is the twenty-ninth anniversary of my birth and it's a mighty solemn occasion. . . . I was so disappointed at not hearing from you today. However, my mama remembered me and I found a nice long letter from her reminding me of the seriousness of the occasion and wanting to know if I was not ever going to get married and in fact entering into quite a long dissertation on the joys of matrimony and of being settled. She doesn't think I am ever serious about girls. If she only knew, dear, how terribly in love I am right now I am sure I would get a world of sympathy from her."

In June 1906, Josephine wired Eugene that she and her mother were to arrive in Los Angeles in two weeks and asked him to look for a house they could lease for the summer. He was overcome with happiness and began at once looking for a place. He found a large one that seemed right and wrote her instructions about sending the trunks and the servants on ahead, so that he and they could get the place in readiness. With her mother as chaperon, he and Josephine enjoyed trips up and down the coast together, and it was indeed a happy summer for the three of them. Later that year, Eugene was transferred to Chicago, where he went reluctantly even though it meant a promotion for him.

Once again the lonely letters arrived in Josephine's mailbox and Eugene was begging her to "come to me for I can't live without my darling baby." Then, in December, he wrote, "This was the happiest day I have known since I left my baby . . . it was real red letter day.. First of all, I had two of the sweetest, dearest letters I have ever received from you dear, and then just after reading them, Mr. S. [T. M. Schumacher, president of EP & SW] called me in his office and asked me to go to the coast to handle the orange business for the EP & SW. And oh! darling, I could have shouted for joy. So I wired you today asking you to get me a nice room and bath where you and Polly [Allie] are going to stay." He was to be in Los Angeles until March and the prospect filled him with happiness.

He and Josephine seemed very close in those days and Eugene had reason to hope that the favors she granted him meant she would soon agree to set the wedding day. But the next year, she drifted away once more and it was not until 1908 that the love affair seemed to be going well again. In January of that year, Eugene was sent to attend a conference of railroad agents at the Homestead Hotel in Hot Springs, Virginia. He wrote Josephine about its beautiful setting, high in the Blue Ridge Mountains, and about the elegance of the hotel inside and out; he declared that he would surely be able to have a good time there if only she were with him. "I'm going to bring you and Polly here some day," he promised. He travelled a great deal in his work. Soon after leaving Hot Springs, he went to Washington, D. C. with some of his railroad associates, staying at the New Willard Hotel. He visited many of the fine government buildings, spent hours in the Library of Congress and met "more senators than I knew existed." He wrote Joe: "There is a reception at the White House tonight and Tom Scott & I were invited by Congressman Cook of Colorado, but Tom didn't have his dress suit so we didn't go. I had lunch today with Senator Guggenheim and Congressmen Cook and Browning, Tom Scott and Chas. Griffith from Colorado. We also had a half hour with

Speaker Cannon in his private office in the Senate. . . . The Speaker is certainly a fine old gentleman. He is seventy-one years old and said today that he would live to be one hundred, and entertained us with several stories." Eugene looked up his mother's cousin, Zac M. Knott, a bachelor who seemed to be one of the society leaders in Washington. "He says if I will bring you to Washington he will see that you are quite the belle of the season. I told him I feared that some one would steal you from me here. Of course he slipped me a very nice compliment." Again, Eugene spoke of how much he wished Josephine were with him and said he wanted to bring her to Washington some day.

The summer of 1908 was a banner season for Eugene, as he managed to get enough time off to accompany Josephine and her mother to Europe. During the crossing, long days on shipboard gave Eugene and Josephine rare opportunities for companionship and their long talks seemed to bring them to a close understanding. Then followed almost a month of new experiences and adventures as the three El Pasoans travelled through Europe. Joe and her mother were safely settled in Paris for the winter when Eugene returned home. Letters were slow and cables expensive, so Eugene had little news of Josephine and Polly and it seemed to him that the winter would never pass. Finally a cablegram came asking if he would meet them in New York, as they were to disembark there in two weeks.

Joyfully, he met their ship, helped them with customs and eagerly awaited news from Josephine about an early wedding date. But he was disappointed again, for her eyes were worse and she told him that she must remain in New York indefinitely for treatment.

An event that surprised and shocked Josephine and Eugene took place in June, 1910 when Allie, who had been in El Paso alone for some time, impulsively married a young man, J. B. Swinney. It had apparently been a whirlwind courtship, carried on in complete secrecy. Eugene arrived in El Paso shortly before the marriage took place and said he and Dr. Brady tried to find the man, but they did not even know his name until the license was issued. Then Allie, fearing Eugene would interfere, moved the hour of the wedding up from evening to noon.

Eugene wrote Josephine about the affair: "I went up to the house about seven last night and met him. You can imagine my feelings, darling. I wanted to beat him to death. I said nothing to him. He said 'I hope we'll be friends.' I said 'that depends entirely on how you treat MRS. CLARDY.' I didn't want to be mean or nasty on Polly's account, but dear I was furious so could not treat him civilly. He has been in charge of the Ready-to-Wear dept. at the Popular. Said he came from Macy's N.Y. . . . He can't be over 30 years old and I am sorry to say it dear but I am sure it can't last always. Of course he is after her money and it seems such a shame that Polly can't see it."

Eugene had consulted the Smith office and Attorney Turney about the state of Josephine's affairs and advised her to take steps at once to protect her interests. She had three pieces of property in her name but much of her support had been coming from her mother. "Polly gave me $150 which I will get & send you or telegraph tomorrow and there is $50 deposited in the State Nat'l Bank subject to your check. It's the rent from the Montana St. house. She said to tell you that was all she could give you and that you would have to come home as she would not keep you in N.Y. any longer. . . . I also wired you today about power of attorney. If you ever gave her one you should revoke it at once, so that she cannot involve any of your property. . . . If you want to come home now, Mrs. Rupert will stay with you at the house. Polly says she won't go there on their return. And if you don't come before they come back I am going to move down to Bassett's." He suggested that if she did not come home, he would meet her elsewhere, either Chicago or at his mother's home in Kansas City to talk over plans and concluded: "I'd give part of my life if I had money enough to take you away from it all and stay away by ourselves where we could be happy together."

That the marriage was a mistake must have become obvious to Allie in a short time, for it was soon dissolved and she resumed the name of Clardy. Quick action on the part of Eugene, the Smiths, and her attorneys had protected her property from the luckless bridegroom, if indeed he had entertained any hopes of financial gain. He apparently faded from the scene, possibly going back to Macy's. And the rift between mother and daughter was soon mended.

Year after year passed from 1910 to 1915 with Eugene still the faithful lover and Josephine reluctant to give up her single way of life. The wedding was postponed so many times that Eugene rarely had the courage to hope it would eventually happen. Business affairs of the Clardys fluctuated, but enough money seemed available for Josephine's travels, and usually Allie went with her. When they were away from El Paso, their home was left in charge of the Chinese cook and housekeeper, Lee, who looked after Mrs. Clardy's little dog, Pupsey. Eugene's work kept him travelling most of the time, and as he wrote sadly, it seemed that he and Josephine were almost always at "the opposite end of the line."

More and more, Eugene was regarded as a member of the family and consulted on business matters by Grover Smith, who handled the Clardy rentals, and by the bankers and lawyers for the Clardys when he was in El Paso and Josephine and her mother were away. In December, 1911, they were at the Astor in New York and Eugene was working out of the St. Louis office. He wrote Josephine that he wanted to get her a fur collar and muff for Christmas, which he wanted her to select. And he asked her to choose a gift for her mother that he and Josephine could give her together.

After a few days together during the holidays, Eugene was again in El Paso on January 6, writing from the Toltec Club to Josephine in New York, at the Waldorf. He was lamenting that trains in the East were snowbound and he had not received her letters. But weather was fine in El Paso, he wrote:

I played polo yesterday and this evening and like it very much. I am riding two of [Charles] Bassett's ponies, so it doesn't cost me anything and I think will do me a lot of good and take my weight down. I think it's a fun sport. Yesterday and today were beautiful days, warm and balmy so I had Lee water the flowers. Don't you think I better have the sash made for the front flower beds now and have 'em all painted green? So they will look nice when my wife gets home. The carpenter, or whatever he is in one of your stores won't pay his rent so they have ordered him out, but don't you worry about business now. I guess he'll come across before moving.

This was typical of Eugene's protective attitude toward Josephine. — he would suffer loneliness, even hardship; would shoulder every worry that he could and when he had to write her about business worries, he even apologized although it was her business, not his. In April 1913, he was in El Paso writing to Josephine at the Waldorf saying:

I arrived home this morning and found your two letters. Am sorry you have been bothered with business affairs. Mr. Smith says he received the deed (which had been mislaid in Turney's office) and closed the trade for your & Grover's property. I saw George [Flory] at noon and had five hundred credited to your acct. as per my wire today. He did not know what your balance was but promised to have a statement made up today and write you tomorrow. George said you needn't have worried, that he would have paid your checks. Smith called me up last week and said Buckler threatened to foreclose on Polly (Allie) if his interest was not paid by Monday, hence my wire to her. Smith paid him last Monday. I was up at your house Sunday and cut a couple of posies and sent 'em to you. Saw Pupsey and she looks fine and acts happy.

There were times when Eugene became very discouraged and felt he and Josephine could not continue a relationship which was so unsatisfactory to him. The spring of 1914 was such a time. Writing from Chicago to Joe (still his "Dear Baby") in El Paso, he said: "I'm sorry dear you are having so many difficulties to contend with and I guess I only serve to add one more to the many." Perhaps this refers to her mother's frequent severe headaches. "This is April and your letters all spell between the lines that your mind is not yet made up. I've about concluded that you have decided that you don't want me. However we can discuss that the next time I see you. I don't know now when that will be but I hope soon. You may be going through here soon. You spoke of getting away as soon as possible and I know only too well in what direction your steps would turn and don't blame you my dear." He means New York, of course, for Josephine still loved that city.

He discussed some land he owned in Ysleta and San Elizario and authorized Josephine to sell it whenever she had an offer of which she approved. He concluded by saying "A man is in a bad way who loses hope. Well dear, we have had a hard struggle to adjust our lives to our liking, haven't we? I know you do the best you can and I am not complaining. Your own heart can tell you what to do and what is best for you. . . . Love to Polly, As ever, devotedly, Eugene"

CHAPTER VIII

The Crisis

~§ JOSEPHINE DID GET AWAY from El Paso and her problems that fall, going to New York where she again took up residence in the Waldorf. Her mother was with her part of the time, but went back to El Paso on business in February. Just after February 14 Josephine wrote to Eugene (who was in California) one of the most affectionate of all the love letters he received from her. She said:

My Sweetheart, I wouldn't have known that it was Valentine's Day yesterday were it not for the beautiful violets and orchids which you sent me. It was lovely dear, and especially sweet of you. . . . I have been to the opera three times since you left, heard Caruso sing in 'Manon.' . . . I went to the Charity Ball with Ex Gov. Colquitt and a Texas girl friend of his — a maiden of uncertain age whom he was seeing home from Paris. . . . Please dear, write to me. I haven't anyone but you in all the world and I love you. Devotedly, Your Own, Josephine.

The above sentences are extracts from a very long, newsy letter, which must have taken much effort, for writing was not easy for Josephine.

While Mrs. Clardy was in El Paso, Margaret Rupert, a friend who kept a rooming house, wrote Josephine saying:

Your Mother found Lee [the cook] with a very sore hand and unable to do the work. He said Pupsey bit him. She went to work cleaning house and got after Grover so everything is in first class condition and in reddiness [sic] to sell.

We had an unusually heavy fall of snow, it was very cold and disagreeable and so Mother stayed here with me part of the time and when she wasn't here, I was up there. . . . Miss Clara Hague phoned yesterday said she was very sorry she did not see your mother before she left. Your Mother left on the Texas & Pacific last night.

Later that year, Mrs. Clardy was again in El Paso and Joe was still in New York, where she was having her portrait painted and spending time with some very interesting and amusing friends. Mrs. Rupert wrote Joe in August, saying she had just returned from California and was suffering from the heat, such a hot spell as had never been "in the history of El Paso. . . . I found your mother looking so well, in fact better & fleshier than I have ever seen her. I have rented the old Patterson building; it won't be ready for six weeks so I will remain with [your] Mother."

About this same time, Josephine received a letter from an El Paso man, Robert A. Martin, who signed himself "Your devoted friend." He had just returned from several weeks in San Francisco and he also was feeling the "fierce heat" of El Paso's summer. He said:

You know how delightfully cool and fresh it is there (in S. F.) in summer. One day Pearl Cartwright Graham and her sister Blanche asked at the St. Francis for me and we had a good afternoon at the Orpheum and at Rex Restaurant dancing and putting away booze. Blanche talked a lot about you — she admires you immensely. When Mlle. Pavlova left San Francisco I gave her conductor Theodore Stier a letter to you and probably by this time he has presented it. He is one of the most charming men I have had the good fortune to know and I hope you will like him. He will ask the Countess Svirskaia to call on you if you wish — she is a great friend of Nazimova and the Countess, who is known here as Countess de Sevirsky is a most interesting woman and some dancer. Let me know how you like Stier.

Robert Martin is said to have followed Pavlova almost around the world, before he met and married a French girl whom he brought back to El Paso to live. Perhaps she and Josephine were friends, but no record exists to confirm it.

Roland Hinton Perry was painting Josephine's portrait that summer and some of the sittings were held at the summer home which he and Mrs. Perry maintained at Richmond Summit, Massachusetts. Their salon included many prominent persons, one of whom was an inventor, Edmund Rousselet (de Castilly), who was enamored of Josephine. He wrote her from New York that he was returning to Richmond in his car to drive her back to the city, after which he sent notes to her hotel inviting her to dinner and the theatre.

Another friend who was paying court to Josephine at this time was Charles S. Thorne, a socialite who also had a car and was taking her out for drives and dinner. He was quite a sportsman and perhaps he was the one with whom Joe rode in the park. A letter is preserved from a woman who said she understood Miss Clardy wanted to buy a side saddle and who had one for sale. Later, when Charles had gone to the Johnson Camp on Moosehead Lake, Greenville, Maine, he wrote Josephine describing it as a "beautiful and wonderful spot." This camp was the retreat of members of the wealthy Johnson & Johnson Manufacturing family.

Josephine was receiving letters from another Charles, one of the Qualey boys of Mexico, well known young men about town in El Paso, whose family were friends of the Clardys from early days. Charles had been seeing Josephine in New York and addressed her as "sweetheart" in these letters written from Kingman, Arizona, where he was apparently working as a mining engineer.

As Josephine was corresponding with two or three other admirers, it is no wonder that Eugene felt sadly neglected.

Finally on August 8, 1915, Eugene wrote to Josephine at the Waldorf, saying:

I have tried to hear from you by long distance and letter for the past two months but without avail. There is only one conclusion left to me and that is the one I have so often told you of before. It is evident that you wish to be free from our engagement. I have felt this since 1908 ever since I learned of your attachment for the little blonde Clarance and more pronouncedly so when you returned from New York to El Paso in 1912. It isn't necessary for me to go into detail. I probably know more about your affairs than you realize.

I am therefore doing what I believe you would wish me to do and what I think you have wanted me to do for a long time. Therefore you are free from our engagement! Please send me my letters at your earliest convenience. I am returning via American express today ALL of yours together with the few personal belongings of yours which still remain in my possession. I am not attempting a long dissertation on the reasons for my actions as I know you know them only too well. If you seek for them, examine your own conscience. You have been unfair.

My one wish and desire for your future is that you may be as happy as you have made me miserable. Sincerely, Eugene

Receipt of this letter from Eugene must have stunned Josephine and brought her to the most serious thinking she had ever done. In her heart she knew that the life she was leading was all froth and fun, and that Eugene was the most solid, real person in her life. She had depended on him for years and had never questioned the sincerity of his love and devotion. Her mother loved him, too, and no doubt would be heartbroken when she learned of this development. "What in the world would I do without Gene?" Joe must have thought, "And what would he do without me? It would probably kill him to give me up. I must get him back right away. And I'll try to make up for all the unkindness and neglect he has suffered by being extra sweet and loving to him. Then he and I and Polly will make a happy home together."

When she told her mother about Gene's letter and her own unhappiness, tears began to flow; it was as if she were a little girl again in her mother's arms. "You must let him know at once that you still love him and that you are ready to marry him," her mother advised. Eugene was in Chicago where Josephine reached him by telephone, and although they had a very bad connection, she managed to convey her message and promised that a long letter would follow at once.

Eugene's broken heart was soon mended and wedding plans went forward. Could it be possible he was finally to realize his dream of marrying his Joe?

Yes, he finally had a firm promise from Joe that the wedding date would be set soon. But Eugene had to wait until his business affairs were taken care of. He had to make a swing that fall throughout the Southwest and on to California. He was in El Paso in October writing Josephine how unhappy and lonesome he was so far away from her. But he was receiving sweet letters from her now and that made him "as happy as a lark" when she told him that she loved him and him only.

In El Paso he had been a dinner guest of his long-time friends, Charlie Bassett and wife. They had been married a few months earlier, and he said, "They have a beautiful home and are very happy." There is news in his letter too of other El Paso friends, Mrs. Clarence (Alexina Fall) Chase and her sister, Jouett Fall, who were visiting the Bassetts. He was sorry to have missed seeing Josephine's mother, who had left El Paso with her maid, heading for New York on the day he left Chicago for El Paso.

For the next month, Eugene was busy in California, writing Josephine from the Fairmont Hotel in San Francisco, later from Hotel Van Nuys in Los Angeles. Back in El Paso in late November, he had a conference with his superior, A. N. Brown, general traffic manager for the EP & SW, who had written him to remain indefinitely in California. Brown wanted him to stay until the citrus crop was all in, which he said would be sometime in February or March. Eugene was able to persuade Brown that it would not be necessary for him to stay, but that he could make another trip to California later on. Eugene was anxious, naturally to get back to Chicago from where he could get over to New York to see Josephine. While in El Paso, he was trying to straighten out his affairs by selling some of his land on which he was paying interest but he said it seemed that he could not "give it away." Also he was having trouble with a Chinese tenant, but he wrote, "I musn't bother you with my troubles, dear, as you have troubles enough of your own."

He promised that he would certainly see her between the 17th and 20th of December and would wire her when he reached Chicago. Things did not work out quite that well for him, but he did get back to Chicago as he had hoped.

CHAPTER IX

With This Ring

ᴌ᛭ JOSEPHINE MARSALIS CLARDY and Eugene Emmett Fox were married very quietly on January 20, 1916 in the Collegiate Church of St. Nicholas in New York City. Probably only two witnesses were present: the bride's mother, Mrs. Zeno B. Clardy, and Eugene's friend, S. S. Crow. A compromise was evidently reached on the religious issue, since Eugene was of the Roman Catholic faith and Josephine was a member of a protestant church. The vows were solemnized by the Rev. Malcolm James MacCleod, minister of the Reformed Church in America.

Preparations for the wedding had started in the fall, after the broken engagement and the reconciliation. Mrs. Clardy had closed her home in El Paso to come to New York for the season and she and Josephine were established in the elegant Idaho Apartments. Mrs. Clardy had really wanted to give Josephine a big church wedding in El Paso with a reception afterward for all their friends. But Joe-Joe had decided several years earlier that she did not want that sort of wedding; instead, she wanted it to be simple. Besides that, it was now war time and belts were being tightened everywhere. However, she and her mother had been shopping for weeks for the trousseau.

As Christmas approached, they hoped Eugene would be in New York to spend the holidays with them. But Josephine came down with an attack of tonsilitis and Gene was caught in the rush of railroad traffic. He wired Joe that he was heartsick about it, but that he would not even get to see her at Christmas — he had to leave December 25 for a swing through the Southwest, then back to Chicago to leave immediately for California. The wedding date could not be set until he got back from the West and made arrangements for the private railroad car in which they were to honeymoon. In the meantime, he wired that he was sending her a Scotch mole coat and muff for her Christmas gift. He asked her to select a gift for Polly from him and to

Private car for honeymoon trip.

buy a doll to be sent to little Mary Schumacher, daughter of his boss, Tom Schumacher.

Eugene got back in mid-January. The wedding day came; the vows were said; Eugene and Josephine were finally man and wife. After the ceremony, there surely was a gay champagne supper for the little wedding party. Then the newlyweds went at once to the special car which Gene had almost certainly filled with flowers for the bride. They waved goodbye to Allie from the rear platform and started on the honeymoon trip that Eugene had dreamed about for almost eleven years. Josephine looked lovely, her mother thought, wearing the elegant coat and muff which Gene had given her.

They went first to Kansas City to visit Eugene's family, then on to California and back, ending their journey in Chicago, where they went to the Blackstone Hotel to reside.

Back in El Paso, the daily newspapers had no information about the wedding except that it had taken place in New York City. The *Times* apparently decided against any announcement, lacking details. But the *Herald*, using a large photo of Josephine from its files, together with a small photo of Eugene, published the following account:

Word has been received from New York City of the marriage of Eugene Fox, assistant general traffic manager for the El Paso and Southwestern Railroad company, with headquarters in Chicago, to Miss Josephine Clardy. The wedding took place on Tuesday in New York and they went to California on their wedding journey. Miss Clardy is the daughter of Mrs. Z. B. Clardy, formerly of El Paso and now of New York, and was a very popular society girl in this city. Mr. Fox was located in El Paso for a number of years and was freight and passenger agent of the E. P. & N. E. railroad company when that company was absorbed by the E. P. & S. W. Since that time he has filled many executive positions, in El Paso, Los Angeles and recently has been in Chicago. Miss Clardy is a talented musician and was spending the season in New York City with her mother. The marriage is a culmination of an El Paso courtship and the news is received in El Paso by the friends of both with much delight. A number of courtesies will be extended to both when they return east from California.

After the wedding, Mrs. Clardy mailed announcements to a wide list of friends throughout the country and abroad. As soon as Gene and Joe-Joe reached Chicago after the honeymoon, they began receiving letters and gifts. One letter came to Eugene from Alexander

Jackson in London, who said, "I note that your persistence finally compelled the handsome young lady to capitulate and I know you are the happiest man in good old Chi."

A socialite friend of Josephine, Isabel F. Hapgood, wrote from New York berating her for not telling her of her plans to be married. She said she had learned of it from friends, "the H's and the P's, who had read it in Town Topics." She said, "Mrs. P. has a weakness for knowing everything and everybody. I remember her telling me that her 'list' included 4,000 people — or was it 7,000? Right here in New York, too, if you please! I went over to The Idaho to see your Mother, but did not find her there, so will write her in El Paso."

After wishing the couple happiness and prosperity, she continued: "Do not let the smoke of Chicago blur your memory of me. If you ever come on here, and it is unthinkable that people should not escape from Chicago to New York occasionally, do let me see you. My address is always in the Social Register, the latest copy of which is always on view at the Hotel Information desk." These were just Josephine's sentiments about Chicago and it was only a short time before she was "escaping from Chicago to New York." She loved New York and during the rest of her life, when it was possible to go there, Josephine was in New York for the fall opening of the opera and new plays.

Another letter with wishes for happiness came from May Perry, wife of Roland Hinton Perry, the artist who had painted Josephine's portrait in 1915. She said they had both been ill and had a dreary time of it, "but I have been happy to think of you in your happiness." She added, "Did you overlook sending Comtess d'Aix a card? The address is Kenilworth, Ill. but they are here at the Waldorf now. I thought you would like me to let you know they did not receive one. His name is Comt Frederic d'Aix — I think they are very fond of you."

For the almost life-size oil portrait painted by Mr. Perry, Josephine had chosen a beautiful blue gown with low decolletage. A filmy scarf reveals her beautiful white shoulders, and the abundant dark hair is arranged in a low bun on her neck. As one looks at this portrait, which now hangs in the Centennial Museum at The University of Texas at El Paso, one can imagine the pride with which Eugene Fox introduced this lovely creature as his wife to his circle of friends in Chicago.

Although Josephine was nearing the age of thirty-five when she was married, in the portrait she has the enchanting, dewey look of a young girl. Indeed, she must have longed to be young forever. Her age was a closely-guarded secret all her life and anyone who even hinted at it, risked her wrath. This secrecy became almost an obsession as she grew older, and it seemed so important that she resorted to little subterfuges to conceal her age. When she died, the physician who signed the death certificate had to guess at her age.

At one time in his courtship when Eugene was begging Josephine to marry him, he had promised her that if only she would consent he would allow her to go back to New York whenever she wished and would not object. So now she was holding him to that promise. Eugene had to make frequent trips out over the line, and as Josephine and he were living in the hotel, it was a simple matter when he left for her to board the train for New York, riding on a pass as the wife of Mr. Fox. Later when Mrs. Clardy became a member of the Fox household, she also was given passes and for many years she and Joe enjoyed the privileges of almost any rail line on which they chose to ride, and even had passes on some ferry and ship lines.

Mrs. Clardy went back to El Paso after the wedding, but kept the apartment at The Idaho which she had taken on a lease of several months. This was headquarters for Josephine when she was in the city, and here she began to store some antique furnishings and other fine things which she was buying for her future home.

About mid-February, Eugene had to go to California again and Josephine went along, staying a while to escape the cold weather of Chicago or New York. While there, she received a letter from an El Paso friend, Laura Yarnall Warren, who wrote asking that Josephine permit her to give a reception or tea in her honor when she arrived in El Paso sometime in March.

I have an accumulation of social indebtedness covering several years and you will simply be an angel of mercy sent to help me out if you will just tell me about what time in March I can count on your being here. It's the sort of thing I love to do and you have so many friends here who will want to wish you happiness. I saw your husband at the train yesterday and he exhibited all a lover's impatience to be off. Also promised to come to my party for you and act as well as Dr. Stark and all the rest of the recent bridegrooms did at their parties. . . . Dick sends you his best wishes and is looking forward to the pleasure of knowing you better.

{ 63 }

Josephine was at Hotel Paso del Norte in El Paso in March when she received a letter from Eugene in Chicago; he had been hoping each day to receive a wire from her saying she was on her way home to Chicago. Mr. Schumacher had been there and had told him that he was to be promoted to general traffic manager, succeeding Mr. Brown.

"I am sorry to have to tell you dear that he insists on me [sic] living in El Paso. I know how disappointing this news will be to you but I can't avoid it and hope that if you see him [he was en route to El Paso] you will not let him know that it will not be pleasant. . . . I have been almost afraid to tell you about it, however it means a great deal to my future." He added that there would be no announcement of his promotion for sixty to ninety days, and closed by begging her to wire him that she was on the way to join him in Chicago.

Josephine loved New York and surely would have been happy to live there, or perhaps in California, but she still thought of El Paso as the little dusty town of her childhood, where nothing amusing or exciting could happen. Actually, the town was growing into a small metropolis, with many paved streets and new buildings. Plans were being made and money raised at that very time for the new Woman's Club building on North Mesa and a few blocks away, St. Patrick's Cathedral was soon to be erected. The Mexican Revolution was also providing much excitement for El Paso residents; the National Guard had arrived and the town was certainly not dull that year.

For business or other reasons, Josephine was still in El Paso in early April when Eugene wrote saying it had been a whole month since they had arrived in El Paso together and he had left her there. "I was so in hopes you would be here today or tomorrow, as I will probably have to go to New York this week and wanted you to go with me. But you know best of course, dear, what you should and want to do."

In another letter a day or so later, he mentioned the fact that an acquaintance from El Paso had called up and asked if he was "the man who was married to Josephine Clardy." He said he had that honor, "but some think it strange that you are not here with me." He declared in this letter his great love for Joe and tells her she is the "most beautiful woman in the world." Then he mentioned again his proposed trip to New York, said how lonesome he was and baited her a bit with this remark: "And besides, there is a pretty hat in the window on Michigan Ave. that I think you'd like."

Perhaps the hat bait worked, for Josephine was inordinately fond of beautiful hats and gained a reputation for wearing the most elaborate, even flamboyant, hats to be found. She went to New York with Eugene and was again settled at The Idaho, where she remained until the move to El Paso later that year.

In late May, 1916 Josephine went for a short holiday to Montreal and Quebec with New York friends, the Jones family. Eugene had been on the road for a few days and upon returning to Chicago, got word that Allie Clardy was in Providence Hospital in El Paso where she had undergone surgery. He was due to make a trip there anyway and left at once for El Paso, after trying to reach Josephine by letter and telegram. He had consented for her to make the trip to Canada, but did not know her exact address, since the Jones family was motoring.

The news of Eugene's appointment had just been made public and he was receiving letters and wires of congratulation. One telegram was from Polly, who was still in the hospital. Brief notes came from George Flory and Charles Bassett in the State National Bank. Charles wrote that if Eugene did not have a place to move into in El Paso, he could use the Bassett home until September, for they would be away for the rest of the summer. How Eugene must have wished his wife had been with him to read these messages as they arrived, and to accompany him to El Paso to look after her mother.

Arriving in El Paso, he found Mrs. Clardy recovering from the surgery and being well attended by doctors and nurses. He wrote Josephine that he was taking Polly flowers every other day and spending each evening with her. He also took along fruit, magazines and anything else he could think of that would cheer or add to her comfort. But she had been a very ill woman and hers was a long, slow convalescence.

On July 20 Allie herself wrote to Josephine from Providence Hospital saying "I know you will be glad to receive a letter written by your little mother." Josephine had been very concerned upon returning to New York, had wired and written her mother and also Miss Cowles, one of the nurses, asking for news of Mrs. Clardy. Of course she had been hearing regularly from Eugene, but wanted further assurance that her mother was really all right. Her letter continued:

I am able to be up and around my room most of the day. Had a little spell for the past two days but am up again today. Miss Cowles laughed and said it was because I missed 'Mr. Fox.' Perhaps she is right, for I do miss him more than I realized. He was so sweet & lovely to me. Came to see me every night, sometimes in the afternoon. . . . I will be so glad when he gets back which won't be long. I am so glad you went to Canada, for I know you always feel the heat. . . . I am so interested in what you are buying — so many beautiful things & I know that when we ever do have a home it will be beautiful. . . . Everyone has been lovely to me, Myra [Newman] especially, comes twice a week. She came the night before the operation and was the first to see me after. . . . Now my little baby girl, take good care of yourself and we will hope the time is not far distant when we will all be together in a home once more.

There were no reproaches for Josephine from either her mother or Eugene. Perhaps it was necessary for her to remain in New York, or nearby, as she was probably still undergoing treatment for her eyes there. Then too it seems that both her mother and husband regarded Josephine as a delicate, flower-like being who could not stand the heat of El Paso's summer weather.

When Eugene got back to Chicago he wrote Josephine in The Idaho recounting his stay in El Paso and his visits with her mother. He said he has told Polly he will take her either to California or to Excelsior Springs, Missouri, to recuperate as soon as she was able. He said she still had pain which he thought was from her liver and he believed the Springs would be better for her. He implied what may have caused her trouble when he wrote: "I believe that she will never drink again as Dr. Brown and Dr. Wright have told her it would prove fatal."

He continued: "I will know Wednesday what my plans are and will wire you. Of course I didn't want you to go to El Paso in the heat. I told you that I wanted you to do as you liked. Naturally I get lonesome. Most any man married seven months and with his wife only two months would not be very happy. But as long as you are happy I can and will bow to the inevitable and hope that everything is for the best."

He said his sister Eva had written that she wanted to go to Chicago to spend the weekend with them, assuming that Josephine was there. But as they had both been away, the message was not received. His father has asked him to go home for the coming weekend (to Kansas City) and while there, he would explain to Eva and hoped she would not still feel hurt.

By Mid-August Eugene was in El Paso trying to get his office organized and at the same time looking for an apartment for Polly. He wrote Josephine that they had found a very nice furnished one, The Rosemont on North Oregon, where he would take Polly and an old lady she had engaged for a housekeeper. He would stay there until Josephine arrived, when they could get a larger one. The house on Montana Street was soon to be vacant, he said, and was in pretty good condition. But he and Polly had to agree to keep the apartment until January 21 after which time they could move into Josephine's house at 1119 Montana if she wished. He said he knew she could make it into a beautiful home with her ideas and taste and the lovely antiques she had been buying. He regretted he could not handle all the details of her moving from The Idaho, but said his new job demanded all his time. However, he wrote her whom to contact and how to get help from his railroad friends and associates, who would handle everything for her.

And so it came about in 1916 that Josephine and Eugene moved from Chicago and New York back to El Paso, where Josephine soon immersed herself in the absorbing task of setting up her own home.

Josephine's house at 1119 Montana street.

CHAPTER X

The Happy Years

JOSEPHINE HAD WORKED HARD to make the Montana Street house into a home of which she and Eugene could be proud. Fine lace curtains hung at the windows; beautiful furniture, rugs, and art objects were placed in the spacious downstairs rooms. Upstairs, a separate apartment was occupied by Mrs. Clardy, while Joe and Eugene were comfortably settled in other rooms and a guest bedroom was ready for visitors. A Chinese cook was in the kitchen, a housemaid did the laundry and cleaning and a chauffeur drove Mrs. Clardy when she went out to visit her properties, riding in her first automobile, purchased about this time.

In the spring of 1917 Eugene's mother and his sister Eva arrived in El Paso for a visit, enroute from Kansas City to California. They went on to San Diego, and were there most of May before Eva found time to write a letter of thanks to Josephine for her hospitality.

In San Diego they were guests of the Burke family, who were being "perfectly wonderful" to them, taking them to see new places constantly. Eva described the visit:

They have a lovely big touring car — thermos bottles and lunch hampers, so we are having big times at the beaches, a new one each time, and yesterday I took my first dip in the great Pacific. My! but it is wonderful. Dear little Mother got her nose sunburned sitting on the sand. She wishes to express her deepest sympathy to you because of your nervous breakdown and hopes that by now you are feeling lots better. You must take that trip to San Antonio and recuperate, for my dear, you're working too hard over that house and if you want to keep well — you must rest from it for a while. Your good health is of more importance than a beautiful home, dear . . . give a big hug and kiss to Eugene for us and keep heaps of love and best wishes for your own dear self. Your loving sister, Eva.

A nervous breakdown is a convenient device whereby a woman may obtain a desired end, such as a much-needed rest or holiday trip. It could prove very useful also to speed the departure of house guests, whose visit might be deemed to have lasted long enough.

In August 1918 Eugene needed a birth certificate in order to obtain a passport, so he could travel on the Nacozari Railroad, of which he was traffic manager. He was at that time general traffic manager of the El Paso and Southwestern System. The Nacozari was a short connecting line, extending seventy-seven miles from Agua Prieta, Mexico, to a mine at Nacozari, Mexico.

Eugene wrote his father, enclosing affidavits to be signed by his parents. "All you have to do is swear that I really was born," he said "and say what relation I am to you and Mother; — also to the fact that I am still alive — at least above the neck." John Fox in Kansas City wrote his son saying he was returning the affidavits, properly executed before a notary as requested. His letter continued:

If the authorities require any further proof of your American citizenship I will gladly furnish additional of same to the effect that both of your grandfathers voted for Andrew Jackson for President of the United States, that one of your maternal great uncles, [Zachary Taylor] who was nick-named by his soldiers "Old Rough and Ready" made the Mexican Army 'sit up and take notice' during the late forties, and that I, your father, served in the Eighth Regiment, Illinois Veteran Volunteer Cavalry, Company G. in

Eugene Fox, general traffic manager of the El Paso and Southwestern System with Dr. James Douglas, president.

{ 70 }

the Army of the Potomac during the early sixties and rode twenty-five miles to cast my first vote for President against U. S. Grant.

Eugene Fox was a capable, hard-working employee of EP & SW, a man who was liked and respected by his superiors as well as those who worked under him. A secretary, Erin Middleton, who worked in his office during the years he had headquarters in El Paso, described him as a fair man, generous and warm-hearted, one who befriended many workmen with whom he made friends while travelling in his territory. "We often saw brakemen, conductors, firemen or engineers come into the office to see Mr. Fox," she said. "If they were in trouble or needed to borrow money, they might be afraid to go to the head of their division, so they would come to Mr. Fox, for they knew he would help them if he could."[1]

Miss Middleton recalled an unusual experience which Mr. Fox related to her. Knowing that she was a musician, he thought she would be especially interested in it. He said that one evening he was sitting in his hotel room in a distant city when he heard somebody playing the violin in the next room. "Now I am not a trained musician like my wife," he said, "but I love music and I know good music when I hear it. I knew this was no ordinary musician playing and when I had a chance meeting in the hallway with my neighbor a little later, I told him that I had been enjoying his music although I couldn't hear perfectly through the wall. I asked him if he would come in my room and accept some hospitality from me and perhaps continue his playing. He accepted and played for me for an hour or more. My guest proved to be none other than the famous Fritz Kreisler, who had generously given me a private recital! It was a marvelous evening and an experience I shall never forget."

According to Miss Middleton, Mr. Fox was fastidious about clothes. He bought his suits from the best-known tailors in New York at that time, Son & Sons, and he paid $250 for a suit. "One time the tailor was in El Paso and Mr. Fox ordered four suits and we wrote a check for one thousand dollars," she said. Eugene had some property of his own and he made a good salary, out of which he supported himself and Josephine. On one occasion, he had heard some gossip about his finances and his wife's money; therefore, he got the office staff together and made an announcement to them. "It is true," he said, "that

[1] Interview, June, 1972.

{ 71 }

my wife is a wealthy woman, her wealth having been inherited. I am not exactly poor myself, but there is a difference, for what I have, I have acquired by my own hard work. But I have never spent one penny of my wife's money, and those who say otherwise just do not know the facts."

He did help Josephine and her mother with business matters, often handling the renewal of notes and such when they were out of town. Many telegrams went back and forth between them about business, but he never made decisions for them. Undoubtedly his friendship with the bankers Bassett and Flory was of great benefit to them, especially when times were hard and money was tight. Mrs. Clardy liked Eugene and appreciated his help, especially in the early years of the marriage. Toward the end of Eugene's life, when he was very hard up and the depression had hurt her own business, she was inclined to blame him for not helping out more at home.

The years passed. Josephine and her mother continued to spend long periods of time away from El Paso, sometimes closing up the house, and then Eugene would move to the Toltec Club. Of if a servant was in the house and a cook to prepare his meals, he would stay at home. When he wrote Josephine about things at home he always referred to the place as "your house," never as "our house." He and Josephine were never blessed with a child, perhaps because she feared motherhood. Friends say that Eugene adored children and longed for a family of his own.

In 1924 the Southern Pacific Railroad bought the EP & SW after much negotiation. When the takeover was final on November 1, Eugene was kept in El Paso at the request of William Sproule, SP president, who had extracted a promise from T. M. Schumacher that he would not take Eugene away. Negotiations had been going on for some time and EP & SW employes were disturbed and uncertain about their futures, so Eugene was probably happy to know he still had a job. Two years later Schumacher, who had bought stock in the Western Pacific, where he was chairman of the executive committee, secured a release from his promise to leave Eugene in El Paso working for Southern Pacific. On October 11, 1926, Eugene received a letter from C. M. Levey, president of Western Pacific, offering him the position of vice-president in charge of traffic with headquarters in San Francisco, effective November 1, at a salary of $14,000 per year.

Eugene was delighted and wired his acceptance. This was another step up the ladder of success in his railroad career. It was an exciting prospect for Josephine, too, as she loved California. Ever since her winter of music study in Berkeley, she had enjoyed visits to San Francisco and still had friends there. Then, too, it meant resuming a pleasant relation with the Schumachers, of whom she was very fond. Terese Schumacher loved Josephine and they enjoyed a warm friendship through the years, as revealed in correspondence which has been preserved. When Josie was in New York, where the Schumachers had a beautiful home, she was invited there for afternoon bridge games and she and Mrs. S. often went to lunch and matinees together. The Schumachers spent many summers at Loon Lake in the Adirondacks. It is probable that Josephine also was invited there for visits, although as a rule she was not in the East during summer months.

Sometimes Terese Schumacher took the girls, Mary and Alice, to California seaside resorts where she would lease a house and bring on a servant or two from New York, so she could have a leisurely vacation during the summer months. And on her way back and forth, she sometimes stopped off in El Paso to see Josephine and her mother.

After Eugene and Joe accomplished the move to San Francisco, there followed three years that were the happiest of their married life. They lived a carefree existence in the Palace Hotel. They were members of the St. Francis Yacht Club and enjoyed sailing; their wide circle of friends made for fun and gaiety and their social life was busy and full. There were concerts and theatres which they both loved and Eugene found satisfaction in his work as a busy railroad executive. Josephine kept her home at 1119 Montana in El Paso, where her mother resided. Whenever Allie became ill or needed her help, Josephine responded by hurrying back to El Paso as she felt a dutiful daughter should. Although Joe loved her mother with a daughter's devotion she also found herself in the role of protector. She had felt this obligation ever since the unfortunate marriage contracted by her mother in 1910. From that time on, Josephine watched her mother's friendships carefully.

Allie Clardy was a charming woman, a good conversationalist and, some thought, an "incessant talker." A longtime friend testified that she was "one of the most charming dinner companions I ever knew." But she was apt to become too convivial at times, so her daughter kept close watch.

CHAPTER XI

Hard Times

✍ EUGENE FOX LEFT HIS POSITION as vice-president of Western Pacific Railroad Co. in 1929 to accept the vice-presidency of the Chesapeake Beach Railway, which operated a short line from Washington, D. C. to Chesapeake Bay. It was proposed to extend the line by means of a ferry across Chesapeake Bay, a venture holding great promise, Eugene thought, but also one which he realized entailed considerable risk. It was backed by a group of influential and wealthy men, however, probably including T. M. Schumacher, executive committee chairman and Arthur Curtiss James, board chairman of Western Pacific, who felt confident that the Interstate Commerce Committee would grant a Certificate of Public Convenience and Necessity for the ferry project.

Their hopes were high and spirits buoyant when Eugene and Josephine arrived in Washington, D. C., and Gene took his wife around to show her the city. He was joined in the ferry venture by his good friend M. J. (Mike) Curry, also a Western Pacific vice-president and the line's assistant treasurer. They were soon so engrossed in setting up appointments and laying plans for their siege of government officials that Josephine wished them luck and departed for New York to visit her favorite haunts.

A few weeks later Josephine and her mother visited in New Orleans and then went on to California for a holiday. There they realized that business was not getting any better and that they needed to return to El Paso to see what was happening to their property. The depression was being felt in El Paso, tenants were unable to pay their rent, and the family income began to suffer drastically.

The year 1931 was one of sorrow and trouble for Eugene and Josephine. Eugene's father died and his mother, ill and grief stricken, was left without adequate financial support. Eugene and his brother Leo, both of whom were in Washington, applied for an increase in Mrs.

Fox's pension as a veteran's widow; with the help of friends, the necessary act of Congress was passed and she received it. Not many years later, a stroke rendered her completely helpless; her two daughters, Gertrude and Eva, took over the nursing duties. Eva Snell lived next door to her mother's home in Kansas City and could go back and forth. But she and her husband had their problems too, including a son in school and two or three dependent members of his family whom he was seeing through the hard times despite his meagre income. Eva herself was suffering from "her spells," as Gertie wrote Eugene, and so Gertie came for long visits to help care for her mother.

Gertrude adored her brother Gene. The farm home in which she and her husband Harvey Harris lived at Dickinson, Maryland, always had the latchstring out for Eugene during his years in Washington. It was a short distance away and he could easily get there for a weekend of rest and relief from his hectic schedule in the city. Gertrude welcomed these visits and could not do enough for "Genie," as she sometimes called him. Harvey, his sister and his mother (who lived in the home) also enjoyed Gene's company and all the family, in Dickinson as well as in Kansas City, were vitally interested in the outcome of his Chesapeake Beach venture.

At Christmas time that year, Eugene managed to get back to El Paso to spend a few days with his beloved Josephine, but his duties hurried him back to Washington and the treadmill of his rounds from one agency to another. Josephine had sent presents to his sisters and their mother. Both Eva and Gertrude wrote letters of extravagant thanks, full of praise for her courage in carrying on without Eugene at home and of her faithfulness and support which meant so much to him in this trying time. They spoke of Eugene's devotion to his lovely wife back home, without whom he "could never have carried on thus far." They judged that Mrs. Clardy was ill a great deal of the time and wished for her speedy return to good health.

It was true that Eugene's devotion to his Joe was still strong, but his letters became less frequent, for he hated to write when there was no good news, or simply no news at all. He allowed time to go by without writing her, hoping that soon he would have something cheerful to say.

In the fall of 1931 the sudden and unexpected failure of the First National Bank of El Paso stunned the city. Businesses and individuals were plunged into desperate circumstances, and the depression which had already been felt in the Eastern part of the country settled with heavy certainty over the city. Across the street, the State National Bank weathered the storm and since it was the bank controlled by Eugene's friends, Bassett and Flory, most of Josephine's business, as well as her mother's, was handled at the State. Thus they themselves did not suffer great loss from the closing of the First National, but it meant hard times for their tenants and for business in general on which they depended for income.

It seemed to Josephine that notes came due faster than ever before and with little or no cash on hand, she and her mother must manage some way to hold their properties together. Sometimes friends came to their rescue; sometimes the sight of two women in trouble softened the hearts of their creditors. A boundary dispute (involving some Clardy property) that went on for years gave them some hope of relief. If they won, the government would pay a good price for the land involved. Eventually they did win, but it was years before the case was settled. Eugene could not help, for he was working without salary.

Day after day during the depression years Josephine and her mother would leave home after breakfast to spend the day in downtown El Paso, according to old friends, and often would sit for hours on the mezzanine floor of the Popular department store. They could watch people on the main floor and often saw their friends among the shoppers. Sometimes they would drop into the nearby real estate office of J. P. McGrath, where they could use the telephone and discuss the sad state of business with Mr. McGrath. He sometimes privately lamented these lengthy visits, saying they interfered with his regular business affairs. He did handle some rentals for the Clardys at this time, although J. H. Smith and Sons had been their principal agent for many years. After the death of Mr. Smith in 1921, his son Grover continued to represent Mrs. Clardy and Josephine in some matters until his death in 1958.

Marshall DeBord, who was handling rentals for Orndorff Realty during the depression, had some property of Mrs. Clardy's at that time. She would call him on the telephone, perhaps about a trivial matter, and talk for hours. Eventually he would put the receiver down, occasionally picking it up to answer yes or no and if the answer seemed wrong, he would amend it. However, he genuinely liked Mrs. Clardy and said she was a lovely lady.

Josephine and her mother had always worn elegant clothes, but as the depression deepened, their garments began to show wear and eventually became almost shabby. Friends recall especially a fur coat that Josephine wore until it looked dowdy indeed. When they were not in the Popular or some real estate office, the two women liked to sit in the lobby of Hotel Paso del Norte, but felt too impoverished to eat in the hotel dining room, often going out to a drugstore for a sandwich at lunch time.

In 1931 still another great calamity befell Josephine and her mother. The house at 1119 Montana was burglarized during their absence and a great many of their beautiful and precious belongings were lost. Many of the lost articles had been wedding gifts to Josephine and Eugene. An inventory had to be taken and estimates of value produced in order to file a claim, a task which Josephine and her mother undertook at once.[1] The claim was filed with Continental Casualty Company by Dexter Mapel, but he has no record of the amount paid. Mrs. Fox told a friend many years later that it amounted to $50,000.00, but this must have been an exaggeration. Sometimes she did like to make a good story somewhat better.

Letters from Hallie Bliss Robinson (mother of Mary Frances Allen, the widow of General Terry Allen) attested to the value of several items. One of her letters (written on November 24, 1931) said:

I recall very well indeed the time, many years ago when the beautiful, talented and charming Mrs. Marie Robinson Wright stopped over on her way from Mexico to New York to visit my cousin Letty, the late Mrs. George W. Emerson. Mrs. Wright was the authoress of a very interesting publication *Picturesque Mexico,* and had been much admired and feted during her stay in the Capital. President Diaz himself, in appreciation of her book, presented her with the national Coat of Arms of Mexico in jewels, and a Spanish shawl, black embroidered in large red roses with deep fringe which you bought from her through my cousin Mrs. Emerson. The shawl, outside of its historical association was in itself unusual, an exquisite type one seldom sees today. What a pity you have sustained such a loss.

Mrs. Robinson was the widow of El Paso Mayor William Francis Robinson, who lost his life while helping firemen fight a downtown

---

[1] Copies of some of the letters they received are among the Fox papers and are of considerable interest.

blaze. Another of her letters to Mrs. Clardy recalled among the lost articles,

your lovely cream lace scarf, the rose point lace handkerchief and perhaps your most prized possession — a black real lace fan which I understood was a gift of a friend and client of Mr. Clardy's in Mexico, and had once belonged to the ill-fated Carlotta, Empress of Mexico. . . . In recalling the old days I am reminded of the close friendship of Mr. Clardy and Mr. Robinson. Our families have been friends for over thirty years. Really as far back as our memory goes on the border.

Maurice Schwartz of the Popular Dry Goods Company placed valuations running into hundreds of dollars on the Persian and Oriental rugs lost; he estimated that lace curtains taken from the windows would cost $200 a panel to replace, that a certain lace scarf was worth $750 and a lace shawl of Point D'Alençon, $1,500.

Several items bought at W. T. Hixon Co. were attested to by J. T. Turner and others from the White House by B. Willmer. A memorandum from Beach Art Shop listing cloisonne vases and other fine objects was signed by Henry S. Beach (whose daughter, Mrs. MacIntosh Murchison resides in El Paso). Another memorandum was signed by Mrs. J. D. Stalker, later known as Mrs. May Stalker White, who presided over millinery at the Popular for many years, during which she ordered Paris and New York original model hats for Mrs. Clardy and Josephine.

An unsigned copy of a letter from a close friend of Josephine's in Guadalajara, Mexico, has some interesting comments about the lost items:

Dear Josephine:

I have understood that the shawls you had with you on your last visit to Guadalajara, the Chinese Ivory Shawl which you then used for an evening wrap, and the embroidered Spanish shawl which you also wore, were the wedding presents of Jimmy Corrigan (of Cleveland) and Fred Fenchler of Juarez, Mexico, and El Paso.

I knew both of these gentlemen intimately for many years. I know, too that they were among your oldest and best friends. Really, Josephine, I don't know that of our mutual friends there were any who had a greater or more sincere friendship for you than Jimmy or Fred. I do not think it is at all to be remarked that Jimmy Corrigan should have given you a wedding present of such value as has been placed upon the Chinese shawl — $2000 or more would not have been unusual for him to have done so. I have never seen anything more beautiful than it was. In the same way I do not think it remarkable that Fred Fenchler should have given you a fine, old Spanish shawl for a wedding present.

I have seen you use a handsome carved fan which I understand was the wedding present of our mutual friend Alberto Terrazas.

Hoping this is the fan referred to and that mother and you are well and happy and with kindest regards to you both.

Sincerely your friend.

In another letter this friend in Guadalajara speaks of trips to Mexico made by Mrs. Clardy and Josephine in earlier, more prosperous times, when he escorted them to various shops where they saw and purchased fine things. These excursions took them to various places including Mexico City. He mentions a time in 1922 or 1924 when they were at the Princess Hotel in the City and Alberto Terrazas and family were stopping at the same hotel. He says:

Not so long ago we were speaking of by-gone days on the border, of the races at Terrazas Park and of many of our old friends. Jimmy Corrigan, Price McKinney A. Terrazas, Fred Fenchler and the sad ending of Joe and Charlie Qualey. You remarked that your three rare, old Chinese vases were brought to you from Mexico and were the gifts of Charlie Qualey. As I remember, they were on the mantle piece in the drawing room. I believe they were given to you 15 years ago at least . . . it was before you were married and during the time Charlie was spending so much time in El Paso.

I remember that several years ago while at dinner in your home the subject of assisting Fred Fenchler in buying a present for a friend came under discussion. Fred wanted you to help him select a drawn work cloth but appeared to be very much impressed with your lace cloth then on the table, asking you where he could get one like it and the probable cost. You answered about $1500, that it had been a wedding present to you and Eugene. He immediately returned to his original idea of buying one of drawn work, saying 'some tablecloth' and laughingly remarked that the next time he won Gran Premio he would get such a one. You felt that the friend in question was justly deserving of as beautiful a cloth as he wanted to give, in that to your knowledge, his cigarettes had destroyed or disfigured the lace and linen of many of her finest ones.

Meanwhile matters seemed to be improving on the Eastern front. After a few weeks in Washington, Eugene was quite encouraged and his letters to Josephine were full of the somewhat ambitious scheme for acquiring the Chesapeake Beach Railroad property (without as he explained, actually having to put up any money), issuing bonds to obtain financing with which to purchase boats and provide operating expenses. When the money was obtained, he said he and Mike Curry would get their salaries immediately. (For the present he was living out of his own pocket.) Prospects looked so good for a while that Eugene was getting bids on repairing the dock areas which had been destroyed by a storm. There were endless rounds of appointments; he was learning that dealing with the U. S. Government was not a simple matter, but involved more red tape than he had ever imagined.

All railroads were suffering from diminishing revenues and many of the smaller lines were in trouble, including Western Pacific. Perhaps this was the actual reason why Eugene left San Francisco. He and Mike knew that Western Pacific had large heavy fixed-interest obligations, which in good times could have been met readily by increased business from the new lines which they had been building in Northern California.

There were rumors that the government was going to create a few railroad groups, merging all lines into them. This would mean that only the stronger lines would survive. "What I went to Washington for was to try and find out for Shu [Schumacher] and James where their properties were going to be placed, but the ICC won't give out anything until they get some action thru Congress," Eugene wrote Joe.

The big financial tycoons in the railroad world were planning to buy up some of the weak lines, Eugene said, hoping to make a profit on them when the time came for the merger. Certainly they wanted to get the best ones, "which show a possibility of earning their way as they would naturally command a higher price when (and if) this time arrives." So Eugene was being asked to make surveys and get information. This required a lot of his time and effort, but his former bosses did not pay him for the work.

He heard that several financiers had formed a company to "buy as many roads as they can as cheaply as possible, then organize a central operating staff to run the roads they own and by such centralization, reduce the cost of overhead. You recall that when the EP & SW was sold, Osborne, Dodge, Douglas and Hawkins all feared it would come sooner than now — and I am convinced it will be in the near future," he wrote.

Almost four years of disappointment and frustration burdened Eugene as he struggled for success in the ferry project. In the midst of uncertainty and endless delays, he was hurt in a taxi accident in 1932 and went to Gertrude's home to spend several weeks recuperating from a broken arm. Discouraged and gloomy, he hated to write to Josephine, and Gertie finally had to explain the lack of letters from Eugene. News of George Flory's death added to Eugene's depressed spirits.

Back in Washington, a certificate was finally granted, then nullified due to the opposition of an existing ferry, the Claibourne-Annapolis Ferry Company, which had strong political ties. The ICC had shifted the matter to the Reconstruction Finance Corporation, whose engineers seemingly approved the Fox request, although their reports were not open to the public. By this time, the functions of the RFC were being taken over by the Public Works Administration and for that reason, the RFC denied the application.[2]

Eugene's funds had run out. He had been living on a meagre budget for many months when in August, 1933, he was offered a job by M. H. Cahill, president and board chairman of Missouri-Kansas-Texas Lines (the "Katy"). He wired Josephine asking for her advice, saying it was not what he had hoped for (he had been negotiating for a job with the CB & Q with some encouragement from Budd). He would have preferred that line, he said, "but I am just glad to get in out of the rain." Gene accepted the Katy offer and within a few days was back at work as traffic manager, the job he knew best, but with a salary only about one-third of what he had made with Western Pacific. His headquarters were in St. Louis and he obtained a room there at the Jefferson Hotel for $3 per day. As he was to travel most of the time, he took the room only for a day at a time. On August 18 he wrote Joe: "Dear Baby — Was so delighted to get your nice letter this morning and I feel like a new man getting back into the harness, like an old firehorse . . . it is fortunate to get anything during these times as so many men with really better qualifications than I are looking for jobs. . . . I love you my baby girl and miss you every minute. Love to Polly, As ever, your devoted, Eugene."

[2] Letter from F. X. Butler to W. H. Bradford, UTEP archives Box 1 FF2.

At this time there was a general impression in El Paso that the Fox marriage was on the rocks — that Josephine and Eugene were separated if not actually divorced. But their letters to each other indicated that the marriage was still sound and that although they were separated in the flesh, in the spirit they were still united.

Eugene was in debt, having borrowed from friends and from Gertrude. He had to leave his trunks at the hotel in Washington, where he said he owed a $300 bill. But as soon as he received his first pay check from the Katy, he began sending Josephine all he could spare. He rode night trains to keep from paying hotel bills, kept his living expenses to a minimum and paid something on his debts every payday.

In October Josephine was hurt seriously when a car in which she was riding overturned. At first she did not write Eugene details of the accident, but when he learned of it, he was alarmed and worried, writing her to wire him if she needed him and he would leave his job and go home. Back trouble, which bothered her for years, probably stemmed from this accident.

Eugene could not get accustomed to the detailed reports required of him; he must report to the office every day as to what he had done, how many interviews he had made and where he would be working the following day. He had been his own boss for so many years, he said, that it was hard to work under such conditions. But he plugged away at the gruelling job, walking miles by day and writing reports at night. He longed to get a few days off so he could go home to see Josephine, but dared not ask for even a day. He was holding on to the hope that Budd of the CB & Q would have a job for him "at least by the first of the year." He hoped he might get back to El Paso for Thanksgiving, but it did not work out. However, a "kindly and sympathetic" boss, Mr. Atkins, called him in to St. Louis in late December and said, "Be sure to come in time to get through so you can go home for Christmas." Oh, what a blessed prospect! Eugene walked on air that day.

CHAPTER XII

Valley of the Shadow

◄§ CHRISTMAS OF 1933 WHEN EUGENE was in El Paso to visit his wife was to be the last time she would see him alive. Three months after the visit, he was stricken on a train and removed unconscious to a hospital in Topeka, Kansas, where he died April 2, 1934. He had been to Kansas City to see his desperately ill mother and to take his turn with his sisters and brother for a few hours at her bedside. Little did any of them realize that his own health was breaking under the terrific strain of the work he was doing and the worry and frustration of the months in Washington. Gertrude wrote Josephine soon after his death: "As he stood at the doorway to leave that last night at Mother's, he said to me, 'Sissy, you and I can not give up. If we cast our hands in the deck, everything is over, so be brave and hold your chin up.' "

Apparently Eugene's death was due to a massive cerebral hemorrhage. Josephine was suffering from damaged vertebra, and had been in bed at home for some weeks when she received the news. Arrangements were made for Leo Fox to accompany his brother's body to El Paso. He remained until after the funeral, and saw Eugene laid to rest in the Clardy family plot in Evergreen Cemetery.[1] Josephine, accompanied by her mother, rode to the services in an ambulance. The short obituary notice in an El Paso newspaper said Eugene Fox had been expected to arrive in El Paso for a visit within ten days.

Difficult times followed for the widow. Theirs had been a strange marriage, marked by many separations. It almost seemed that their devotion was greater when they were apart than when together. In the early days of the marriage, when they were living in El Paso, neighbors sometimes spoke of hearing violent quarrels in the house at 1119 Montana. They said that when Josephine was angry with Eu-

[1] Mrs. W. C. Barnes says her husband and Charles Bassett paid for Eugene's funeral because Josephine was destitute. Interview November, 1972.

gene, she would call into play an amazing vocabulary of fishwifely invective. Then passions would subside and all would be serene again. Such emotional fireworks must have served as an escape valve, as in many marriages when two people are trying to become adjusted to each other. Apparently Josephine was never interested in the house-wifely arts and really seemed unable to find contentment in long periods of companionship with Eugene, although there is no doubt that she loved him in her own way.

As for Eugene's feeling for Josephine, it was pure devotion from first to last. He once wrote her that he saw in her his "Ideal Woman" and he carried this vision with him to his grave.

Although they had been apart many times and had seen each other very little during the last four years, for Josephine there had always been the sustaining knowledge of Eugene's love and protection. His courage had helped her face many difficulties and she had found new strength herself in helping him through the trying times in Washington, even though she remained in El Paso. Straitened finances and her duty to her mother compelled her, she felt, to stay at home.

Now that Eugene was gone, she felt very much alone in the world. Ill and distraught, she began to distrust Eugene's family and seemed to fear that they might circumvent her in getting control of his estate. Gertrude's letters to Josephine through the years had indicated great love and admiration for her brother's wife, not only on her part, but on the part of all the Fox family, and Josephine seemed to reciprocate those feelings. She knew, however, that Eugene was a very loving son to his invalid mother and that he had been very close to Gertrude.

Lying in bed at home, Josephine, who had been named executrix of Eugene's estate, called Attorney Will Burges to come to see her; she also summoned W. C. Barnes of the Southern Pacific office, both of whom she questioned about Eugene's affairs, expressing her fears to them. It embarrassed them and finally they would no longer go to her house but would ask Miss Middleton to go and see if she could be of any assistance to Mrs. Fox.

Eventually her fears were quelled and things seem to have been righted between her and the Fox relatives. George Atkins, the MKT vice president in St. Louis, and others in his office were kind and helpful. Eugene's trunks and personal effects were being held at the Jefferson Hotel in St. Louis, where his bill was unpaid. It was revealed that the hotel manager had contemplated dealing with Gertrude Harris in the matter, but not until the proper legal papers were produced. He did not indicate that she had ever asked him for Eugene's effects. After Josephine's authority was established and she had made a payment on the hotel bill, the trunks and other effects were shipped to her. She had been especially anxious about Eugene's safety box at the Jefferson, but was assured that nobody had access to it but Mr. Fox himself and that he had last made entry to the box on August 31, 1933.

A few months after the funeral, Leo Fox wrote Josephine offering his services in any way that would be helpful. He said he understood his brother's effects were "scattered all across the continent." Leo was out of a job, had been without work for almost a year and had just had another disappointment when a promised job failed to materialize. He asked for a few of Eugene's things, including his shotguns, fishing tackle, riding boots and watch. He said he and Gertie both believed Eugene had named his mother beneficiary of some life insurance.

Eugene's financial situation had been so bad at the last that he had borrowed from friends, business associates and from Gertie. He had borrowed to the limit against his insurance, but had started paying up these debts as fast as he could when he went to work for the MKT Railroad. Had he lived longer, no doubt he would have been able to get his debts paid, especially as there was a much better job promised him for the near future. It was many months before Josephine got all the tangled affairs straight.

At Christmas in 1936 Josephine sent some of Eugene's clothes to Harvey Harris in Dickinson, along with gifts for Gertrude. She did not know that Gertrude had not returned to Dickinson after the long vigil at her mother's bedside, but had stayed in Kansas City. A divorce had been obtained and Gertrude had then married a childhood sweetheart, J. B. Dolsen, whom Harvey described as a "very nice man." About the time Josephine received Harvey's letter of thanks, she also had a long letter from Gertrude, detailing all that had occurred, explaining: "Harvey and I agreed we could no longer be happy together. However, we still remain the best of friends. In fact, he drove back to Kansas City with me when I returned early last winter." She begged Josephine to understand and said she was still grieving over Gene's death and "would give anything if I were only close enough to talk to you about it." She told Josephine she still loved her and always would.

One stroke of good fortune came Josephine's way at this time, when she heard her name announced on New Year's Eve, 1935 as winner of "Bank Night," a prize of a large sum of money. One friend recalls that Josie and her mother were sitting at a small table in the ice cream parlor off the lobby of the Plaza Theatre, which had been conducting the drawing over a period of months, awaiting the announcement. Some friends said "they were so hard up they couldn't afford to buy tickets to the show." Many persons recall the event, but their memory of the amount varies from something like a few hundred to three thousand dollars. At any event, it came at a propitious time, for Josephine had just received a letter a few weeks earlier from the city tax collector, saying he had been empowered to collect all taxes due the city "without discrimination" and advising her that taxes were delinquent in the amount of $1,204.65 on a certain piece of her downtown property. Friends said that Josephine took the prize money and hurried to pay these taxes, thus saving some valuable property. News of her good fortune was broadcast on radio and she received many letters and phone calls of congratulation. One of the letters was from Eugene's thoughtful friend, George Atkins.

Business conditions in El Paso began to improve with President Roosevelt's New Deal. Many jobs were created through the Civil Works Administration and its successor, the Public Works Administration. The River Rectification program for the Rio Grande, about which Eugene had been very concerned while in Washington, had finally got under way a short time before his death. The economy was stimulated further by an influx of troops to Fort Bliss, which brought large payrolls to the city.

Josephine and her mother at last began to see their affairs improving and found themselves able to make payments on some of the notes which friends had been renewing for them during the depression. One good friend, Eda Lochausen Kimbrough, whose husband was R. B. Kimbrough, an officer of the City National Bank and later of the City Mortgage Company, told younger members of her family in later years that she had made loans which "saved Josephine from going broke during the depression."[2]

2 Interview with Mildred Lochausen Myles and Woodruff Lochausen, January, 1971.

Six years after Eugene's death, Josephine lost her mother. Allie Davis Clardy died March 23, 1940. Her funeral service was conducted by the Rev. Paul N. Poling, and pallbearers were Jim F. Hulse, Ballard Coldwell, Grover Smith, Charles Newman, Mason Pollard and Bill Hawkins. Named as honorary pallbearers were Volney Brown, Winchester Cooley, C. N. Bassett, W. H. Burges, Maury Kemp, Robert Holliday, W. C. Barnes, Tommy Mason and Roy Davis.

A woman of great charm, Allie Clardy had many friends in both high and low places. Among her papers was found a copy of a letter she had written to Hugh C. Wallace, whom President Wilson appointed Ambassador to France in 1919.[3] Allie and Hugh had grown up together in Lexington, Missouri, and apparently kept in touch with each other through the years. Her letter was written to thank him for copies of French newspapers and magazines he had sent her, containing his pictures and reports of an address he had made at the dedication of a war memorial.

Among her friends in New York was Mrs John Ringling, who invited her for a visit to the family estate in Florida. In California, one of her good friends was Charles G. Johnson, state treasurer, who wrote Josephine upon hearing of Allie's death: "The companionship between your dear Mother and yourself was something that was very beautiful and sacred. You can always treasure the thought that you made her life happy and contented . . . and be grateful that God gave you such a wonderful Mother."

Allie Clardy was not a social leader in El Paso, but she counted among her friends most of the prominent families and civic leaders of the city whom she had known during a span of almost sixty years spent in the town that was a mere frontier village when she came. But she also liked and counted as friends many persons who were not prominent, including those who served her by bringing ice, milk or mail to her door. These friendships may have caused a few raised eyebrows, but Allie did not mind.

Josephine and her mother had been inseparable for many years and their relationship had been especially close while Eugene was away in Washington and after his death. Now that her mother was gone, Josephine was truly alone, an orphan without chick or child to comfort

3 Wallace later became a chief representative of the United States in Versaille Treaty matters, according to *National Encyclopedia of American Biography*, XCIII.

her. But she had many loyal friends; and when she felt she just could not bear the emptiness of the big house at night, she would ask one of them to come and stay with her.

One of those who spent nights with Josephine was Maria Martinez, who worked for R. T. Hoover & Co., a cotton brokerage firm. Maria, who spoke Spanish fluently, handled the affairs of the tenant farmers who worked on the cotton farms of the Lower Valley land owned by the Clardy family. Josephine would spend many daytime hours in the Hoover office, sitting in a chair by Maria's desk. She was usually wearing one of her big hats and carrying a big black purse, without which she was rarely seen in public. The big purse is said to have been filled with a jumble of business papers, notes about farm matters, notes which Josephine habitually wrote to remind herself about appointments and errands, as well as cosmetics, a few items of jewelry and other trivia such as women usually carry around in a purse. But when she needed to find an important paper during one of the sessions at Maria's desk, it was amazing how quickly Josie could rummage through the mass of papers and come up with the right one. They became good friends and Maria did many personal errands and favors for Josephine, even during business hours.

Others in the Hoover organization were very kind to the widow, including the head of the company, Robert T. Hoover himself. He and his wife were fond of Josephine and she was sometimes a guest in their home. In return, she sent them many beautiful gifts, according to Mrs. Hoover's sister, Mrs. Charles O'Hara.

It seems a fitting coincidence that now most of the oil paintings and many fine art objects and furnishings from Josephine's home have been placed in Hoover House, the official residence of the president of The University of Texas at El Paso. The home for many years of the Hoover family, this beautiful mansion was given to the University by Mrs. Hoover in 1965, a few years after the death of her husband. She moved into a smaller home nearby where she lived until her death in December, 1967.

In 1944 Josephine had Attorney Volney Brown draw a will in which she left the bulk of her estate to The University of Texas at El Paso. A few friends were remembered in the will, such as Eda Kimbrough, Ollie Lansden, Grover Smith and Gus Pundt, but as these friends passed away, one by one, the bequests were cancelled. A sum of money was in the original will for Frances Vance, widow of Dr. James Vance, and Maria Martinez was to receive the home on Montana Street. But when Frances married Serene Durling and Maria became Mrs. Barry Pennington, these bequests were cancelled, perhaps because Josephine felt these good friends were well provided for. For some reason, a bequest to Southwestern Children's home was cancelled, so eventually the sole recipient of the estate was the University.

A few years after Allie Clardy's death, Josephine began to cast about for a suitable memorial to her mother. During the war, the price of cotton had gone up and her affairs in general had greatly prospered; she was prepared to pay well for the memorial. She had found nothing that suited her desires in the matter until 1951, when St. Clement's Episcopal Church built a chapel, named for the builder, Robert E. McKee, an outstanding citizen of El Paso and a staunch member of the congregation. Stained glass windows for the chapel were being designed and built by the Jacoby Studios in St. Louis "with superior craftmanship and every regard for the ancient method and material of the Gothic Masters."[4]

Josephine was allowed the privilege of giving the altar window, which occupies almost the entire East wall of the chapel, in memory of her mother. Mr. McKee, who was to have donated this window, yielded the honor to Josephine and gave the opposite window in the West wall. A small bronze plaque at the lower left of the East window states that it is the gift of Josephine Clardy Fox as a memorial "to my mother, Allie Davis Clardy."

Mr. Lea says, "The use of colored glass to form designs in window spaces is an art peculiarly Christian, born in the building of great cathedrals a thousand years ago. By this art, reverent men have fashioned visible symbols of their approach to God, and brought these symbols to a luminous and mysterious life by the living light that shines down from the sky."

The central figure in the East Window in McKee Chapel is that of "Jesus Christ, in His configuration as Teacher, right hand upraised in benediction, left hand holding an open book displaying the Alpha and Omega symbolizing Christ as the beginning and the ending, encompassing all truth and all enlightment."[5]

4 Tom Lea, *The Stained Glass Designs in McKee Chapel of St. Clement's Church*, El Paso: Designed by Carl Hertzog, 1953, p. 1.   5 Ibid. p. 2.

How comforting it must have been to Josephine, who had been brought up in the Christian faith and had always loved beauty, to know that she had at last found a fitting memorial to the "little mother" who was enshrined in her heart.

In 1956 Josephine gave a tract of land in East El Paso, consisting of about 4-1/3 acres, to the Board of Trustees of the Independent School District of the City of El Paso, for a school located at 5508 Delta to be named in memory of her father, Zeno B. Clardy. She did not erect a monument to her mother or to Eugene, but left money in her will for monuments to them and herself. After the death of Volney Brown, one of the law firm partners, Eugene Smith, handled matters pertaining to her will and it was he who acted as probate attorney when Mrs. Fox died. El Paso National Bank was named executor of her estate in a codicil which she signed in 1965, replacing The State National Bank which had been named executor in the 1944 will.

CHAPTER XIII

Friends and Countrymen

⤷ FOLLOWING HER MOTHER'S DEATH IN 1940 Josephine Fox began to develop into a person known for herself alone. She was no longer in the shadow of her mother, no longer a sheltered and protected daughter, but a woman of the business world, as well as a woman taking her place in the artistic and social circles of El Paso. During the years of World War II she participated actively in war work, bought Victory Bonds and attended the Bundles for Britain and America affairs held in the International Museum. The museum was the former home of Judge and Mrs. W. W. Turney, a stately Colonial mansion at 1211 Montana Street, only one block from Josephine's home.

Josephine often confessed frankly that she "liked men better than women," and there was rarely a time when she did not enjoy the attentions of one or more men friends. But she had some loyal women friends, too, and if they gave her some special attention, she was very warm in her appreciation. One of these was Mrs. Ollie Lansden, society editor of the El Paso *Times,* in whose personal column "Around Town" the name of Mrs. Eugene Fox appeared with some frequency. All who remember Josephine mention her hats, for which she had an unrivalled reputation in El Paso. It is said that when she wore a new hat, if it was not mentioned in Ollie's column, she counted the day lost, and might even be so disheartened that she would return it to the store and look for another.

El Paso was small enough in those days of the 1940s that the social set was fairly limited and someone like Josephine or Ollie could "know everybody worth knowing in town." A typical report of a party is found in Mrs. Lansden's column of June 1, 1944 as follows in part:

Reception and dance which Mr. and Mrs. Sam Watkins gave Tuesday evening to honor their daughter, Mrs. James S. Huff and Lieutenant Huff who are here for a visit was the outstanding social event of the early summer calendar.

The party had the El Paso Country Club as its setting and an orchestra played throughout the receiving and dancing hours.

Mrs. Robert H. Oliver, wearing a shell-pink frock with brilliant clip at the shoulder, greeted guests at the entrance of the clubhouse and the reception line included Mr. and Mrs. Watkins, Lieutenant and Mrs. Huff and the lieutenant's parents, Mr. and Mrs. H. P. Huff.

Mrs. Watkins chose a white and gold costume. Her daughter was gowned in satin and net just the color of candlelight and lovely with her dark eyes and hair. Her corsage was of orchids.

Mrs. H. P. Huff wore a lovely, graceful frock of white chiffon embroidered in silver.

Mesdames Joe Heid and Jack Kaster were presiding (at the punch bowls) while we were there. Zilpha (Mrs. Heid) wore a charming white crepe frock with gold accessories and her ornaments were gold and ivory. Susan (Mrs. Kaster) was in a smart print gown.

Zellah (Mrs. Ed Heid), costumed in a shirtwaist frock of crimson and ivory, was wearing a lovely new diamond dinner ring, gift of her husband.

Mrs. Joe Goodell wore a pretty jacket costume of chartreuse and black.

Mr. and Mrs. H. Arthur Brown, Miss Mary Weeks and Lt. Jerry Sully came together. Mary was wearing a gown of sea foam green, gemmed all over with rhinestones and gardenias in her blonde hair.

Joteen (Mrs. Brown) chose black taffeta designed with frost-white lace jacket. Her coiffure ornament was of gardenias.

Mrs. Paul Thomas had a froth of embroidered mousseline outlining the square decolletage of her black crepe gown. Mrs. Porter C. Thede wore sky blue chiffon and lace; Mrs. H. G. de Portearroyo also wore a blue chiffon frock.

Mr. and Mrs. Charles O'Hara were there, Ruth (Mrs. O'Hara) wearing a charming frock of green and cream chiffon.

Mrs. Eugene Fox was lovely in a gown of black lace designed with long sleeves and slight train and a wide black hat having trim of black paradise aigrets. She wore diamonds and a bracelet of carved jade.

Mrs. George Matkin, who wears her gowns with grace and charm, chose a Roman stripe chiffon frock for the occasion and Mrs. B. M. G. Williams wore a frock of print in which maroon and blue were predominant tints, with pendant of sapphires.

Mrs. Carrie Fant was as beautiful as a portrait in a black crepe frock ornamented only with a cluster of flowers at the side drape. Her pompadoured hair had oranment of orchids, gift of her son Jack Fant, who is overseas.

Mrs. Margaret Schuster Marshall wore black lace and chiffon while her sister, Mrs. Regina Schuster Rabb, was charming in a sea green crepe.

Other well-known names mentioned included Mrs. Camille Kibler Craig, Mrs. C. O. Rucker, Mrs. W. E. Vandevere, Mrs. E. M. Pooley, Mrs. Charles Leavell, Mrs. William Piatt, Mrs. C. C. Covington, Mrs. Virgil Traylor, Mrs. Frances Wooten Aldridge and daughter (Betty Scott), Mrs. L. N. Nickey and Mrs. L. C. Merrill.

Ollie Lansden, who had been a widow for many years, had a special friend and escort, Gus Pundt, whose courtly manners and unselfish devotion to friends won the admiration of all who knew him. Gus spent his life serving his church, St. Clement's Episcopal, and doing good deeds for his friends. Ollie introduced him to Josephine Fox and thereafter the two women more or less shared his attentions, going about either separately or together in his company. When Josephine was out of town, Gus looked after many of her affairs, checking on her house, the mail and so on, then sending her regular reports.

Toward the end of Ollie Lansden's life, she became ill and almost blind. She lived alone in a small downtown hotel and had no one to look after her except Gus. He checked daily on her and remained as friendly and attentive as ever. Often she appeared on the street in a very unkempt state, in contrast to her former meticulous appearance. Only a few friends remained loyal, trying to cheer and help her in any way they could. One of these was Loraine Moore Williams, who had been a fellow-staffer at the El Paso *Times*.

Gus and Loraine never appeared to notice the spots on Ollie's clothing or the uncared-for state of her hair, but Josephine apparently could not bear to see her in this sad condition. One day Loraine took Ollie to lunch in the dining room of Hotel Paso del Norte. To her dismay, when she and Ollie passed the table where Mrs. Fox was seated, Josephine turned her head and motioned them to pass on by, as if she did not wish to recognize her old friend Ollie. When Mrs. Lansden died, she left half of her small estate to some cousins in Kentucky, the other half to Gus Pundt. A sick man himself, Gus survived her by only a few years.

Both Ollie and Gus were mentioned in Josephine's will, which was written in 1944. To Ollie she left only a pretty silver and enamel dresser set, to Gus, her automobile. A Chinese jade lamp was left to May Stalker White, the hat buyer at the Popular, and the income from some business property to Grover Smith. Because all these persons pre-deceased Mrs. Fox, the bequests were cancelled in codicils to her will.

Josephine's gift of $1,000 to the building fund of Southwestern Children's Home was gratefully acknowledged in 1950 in a warm letter from the Rev. B. M. G. Williams, who was then president of the executive committee. In September, 1951, he wrote another letter asking her to be a special guest at the open house and dedication of the new buildings, saying "I want to take this opportunity to thank you so very much for all you have contributed to the erection of this beautiful home."

There were several men in Josephine's life at this time. She sometimes went to parties at Fort Bliss with Jane and Dick McMaster, escorted by a visiting colonel or general, or some other unattached officer. Not knowing how formal the party would be, Josephine would ask Jane, "Shall I wear the first string or the second?" This referred to her diamond bracelets, which she was acquiring with her new prosperity. Her beautiful gowns and jewels were equal to any occasion.

An El Paso man who frequently escorted Josephine was Raymond Dwigans, who was many years her junior but enjoyed her wit and urbanity. In 1961 he was to be named collector of customs at El Paso by President John F. Kennedy. At that time Lyndon B. Johnson was serving as vice president. He and Dwigans had been roommates at San Marcos Academy in Texas in 1926.[1] Raymond had come to El Paso to play football at the then College of Mines, now The University of Texas at El Paso. He knew both Mrs. Clardy and Josephine and when he left college in 1933 to enter business, he leased property on Concepcion Street from them. After Mrs. Clardy's death, Josephine often talked to him of her sorrow and found him a sympathetic friend. She began thinking of making a will and discussed with him the possibility of leaving her property to The University. He encouraged her to do so.[2]

Other men figured in her life, including two who claimed titles, Count Ivan Podgoursky, a white Russian living in San Antonio, Texas, and Count Louis von Cseh of New York. Both sold her paintings and

1 El Paso *Times,* September 26, 1961.
2 Interview with Raymond Dwigans, May, 1973.

art objects for which she paid large sums and which later were appraised at a fraction of their cost.

A man for whom Josephine had great affection and admiration appeared on the scene about 1945. He was Carleton Smith, director of the National Arts Foundation, a highly literate, widely traveled man of the world. Born in 1910 in Bement, Illinois, he held degrees from two universities and an honorary doctorate from a third, his fields of study including economics as well as the arts. He attended the Foreign Service School in Washington, D. C. and the London School of Economics. His research included work in the libraries of Moscow, Berlin, Geneva and Paris.

To get material for his lectures he went to Africa to interview Dr. Albert Schweitzer, to India to meet Jawaharlal Nehru, to the Kremlin to talk with Joseph Stalin, and to Finland to see Jean Sibelius. He learned from George Bernard Shaw, Sir Lawrence Olivier and Queen Mary in England and from Julius Robert Oppenheimer and Albert Einstein at Princeton. He was photographed escorting Mrs. Cornelius Vanderbilt to the opening of the Metropolitan Opera, and on another occasion was a guest, along with Mary Garden, of Governor Adlai Stevenson in the Executive Mansion in Springfield, Illinois.

Carleton Smith came to El Paso as a lecturer on the Town Hall

IVAN PODGOURSKY   CARLETON SMITH

series, for which Mrs. Hallett (Mom) Johnson was booking agent. Mom invited her good friend, Mrs. Fox to a small party for the speaker. It was here that the handsome, youthful visitor from Bement met the middle-aged Josephine and it seemed that a miracle happened. Each saw in the other qualities for which his spirit had been longing and an almost magical relationship was established. It was to last for many years, nourished by an occasional meeting and by notes and letters which "Bambino" as Carleton signed himself, sent to Josephine from all parts of the world. Since each was without a single close relative, he called her his "Other Orphling." When they did meet, they would talk for hours about music, the arts, their mutual love for beauty, and perhaps about the mystery and wonder of the universe and of life itself.

Early in their friendship, Josie had bought and presented to Carleton a plate inscribed with the oft-quoted words from the Book of Ruth," "Entreat me not to leave Thee." He hung it on the wall of his home in Bement where, when not traveling he lived alone. He wrote her from Bement:

Being alone in a big house, which you do too, is no good. People come in but I eat alone and I am very, very sad when I play the piano and no one is here. I think of the many wonderful times we had in New York and wish we were together. The start of our series [this year] is very auspicious. Newspaper men have come from far and wide and I have a room full of clips. But it is all empty without the warmth and presence of My Other Orphling, Josie. On the wall the plate says 'Entreat Me Not to Leave Thee.' Carleton

It seems unlikely that they ever contemplated marriage, but friends say it came as a shock to Josephine when Carleton married Miss Anne Boireau of Paris, France, in February of 1957. After the formal church wedding in New York and a small breakfast in the Waldorf-Astoria, the couple departed by plane for a visit with Pablo Casals, cellist, at his home in Puerto Rico, and later toured South America.

His marriage, however, did not stop the letters Carleton wrote Josephine, although they became far less frequent. On December 10, 1957, he relieved the nervous tension of an expectant father by writing her from the lobby of the New Rochelle Hospital, where he was sitting alone, he said, "waiting for news from Anne and our baby. Fathers seem to be the most useless in these hours . . . my thoughts

turn to you, my only family and the person who understands me best."
He praised Anne as a wonderful human being, sensitive to music,
art, architecture — impressed by nothing external — an idealist but a
hard worker.

I hope you can come soon to see us — and to know your younger Bambino. I read every word of your letter to Tiffany's and saw between lines
the good times you had in Dallas with Callas & the opera. Maybe you can
come to the Met before Easter. Some of the singing is very good, especially
de los Angeles. Every Saturday I shall be listening to the broadcasts with
you. . . . My heart and my thoughts are full in these hours, awaiting a new
life I have helped to create. And I am so glad you are in this world & understand & love, Your Bambino.

Flying American Airlines en route to Washington, Carleton wrote
Josephine on January 18, 1959:

My dear Josie: The world takes on a different shape from the high planes
— and I am thinking of you in the house I've never seen — dreaming of life
and of the future. Word has just reached me that 'Mom' Johnson has died.
I'll always be grateful that she brought me to El Paso & to you. It is not
good to lose contact for we are on this earth all too short a time — we pass
away — where? I see new life coming — our second baby will come to us
in April. Christopher is active, everywhere — curious. We'll be in New
York until June 15th at 50 Sutton Place South. Please write Your Bambino.

What a friend, and what an enduring friendship it was!

Another great and good friend of Josephine's was Mrs. Hallett
(Mom) Johnson, who made a precarious living as a concert manager
for many years in El Paso. In the Spring of 1953 she booked the Boston
Symphony Orchestra for a concert in El Paso Coliseum. Charles
Munch and Pierre Monteux were the conductors. Josephine, thinking
it a good occasion to entertain friends and also wanting to help Mom
meet the very large guarantee for the orchestra, bought a block of
tickets and sent them to friends. But when the evening came, she was
not on hand, having been called to New York for a special event of
great importance. It was the announcement that she had been named
to the Advisory Committee of the National Arts Foundation.

After the concert Gus Pundt wrote her that he had stood at the
door and showed her telegram of regret at being absent to each and
every one of her guests. Gus said, "I am sorry you have not been feeling so well but do hope by now you have fully recovered and that you

are taking in the Big City. I do want to thank you for the concert. I have never heard better. Your guests were most sorrowful over your not being able to be with them and that you had to forego such a grand treat. . . . I am enclosing a clipping from the paper which will give you an idea of how well it was received. . . . Eda and Woody [Lochausen] both said it was OUT OF THIS WORLD, so you can judge for yourself. Mom has just shown me the piece from the New York *Times* about the concert that Carleton Smith sent her."

Mom herself wrote Josie a chatty, breezy account of the concert which apparently was a financial disappointment, although a great musical success. She said:

Josie, you missed the concert of ALL concerts and the very sweetest conductor on the market. . . . Munch was a dear. . . . Your party was a great success and they all missed you. As for my part of it . . . well it was not so good, and just as I said before EL PASO CAN GET THEIR GREAT MUSIC WHERE THEY MAY AFTER THIS. . . . I am going to bring circuses which I can sell for 2.00 . . . that's about their stride for music. As for my coming up, I can't do anything about when until I hear from Marion Evans, who is expected any day now but I think I am coming. When does Carleton leave New York and when are you leaving also?

Margaret and Ralph [Gen. and Mrs. Ralph Meyer] and Regina Rabb [Margaret's sister] had a perfectly lovely supper for Munch and Judd the night before the concert as they got in that night. Munch said he would go and stay five minutes, but with the gals so pretty and dressed up and good food which he said he couldn't eat (but did) and the beautiful things in that house, he was the last man out. He never had been to see us in action, had he? Then after the concert, they all came up to my apartment and waited for the train, which didn't leave until 1:30 a.m. Herndon and Helene [Mom's son and his wife] came to the front and we had quite a party, although not planned. Monteux didn't leave the train, but Munch, Judd, Taubman (N.Y. Times), Rogers of Christian Science Monitor, a French officer and wife, a couple from Mexico City, the Meyers, Regina Rabb, and some others I can't remember, and we had a grand visit with them and a "little" Scotch and Bourbon, cokes, etc.

Well, I hope you are having the time of your life and I will let you hear from me, IF AND WHEN I can come . . . and don't take my boy friend COMPLETELY away from me . . . but Munch is my latest!!! But I don't forget my old and true ones. . . . Loads of love and kisses, and hope to see you . . . when, No se.

Sincerely, Mom.

Josephine had missed the Boston Symphony concert because Carleton had called to say he had some very special plans for her in New York. On May 30, announcement was made there that she had received the signal honor of being named to the Advisory Committee of the National Arts Foundation. The announcement was made by the Foundation president, Millard J. Bloomer, but surely Carleton had nominated her for the post.

Josie was in New York for a month during which she attended a Republican $100 dollar-a-plate dinner along with 4,000 other guests in the Waldorf-Astoria and the Astor Hotels, at which President Eisenhower was the speaker.

She visited the National Art Gallery in Washington and attended the Bach Festival at Bethelehem, Pennsylvania, in the company of Carleton Smith. She saw many of the season's Broadway plays and attended opera and ballet at the New York City Center.

Mom Johnson did arrive in New York, as she had hoped, and Josephine honored her at a birthday luncheon in the St. Regis Hotel. When the time came to return home, Mrs. Fox made her first cross-country trip by air and found it most pleasant, despite her pre-flight qualms.[3]

In her role as concert manager, Mom Johnson often brought musical events to El Paso even though, as with the Boston Symphony, she knew she could not break even. According to her daughter, Mrs. Sherod Mengel, "Mother just would not lower her standards. An organist herself, she was brought up on great music and she always wanted El Paso to have the finest. Consequently she was always struggling to get out of the hole."

One of Mrs. Johnson's regular activities was managing the series of Community Concerts, organized and supervised from a national headquarters. The concerts were open only to season subscribers and a week-long intensive drive was held each spring, after which membership was closed. Volunteer workers, of whom Josephine Fox was one, sold memberships to their friends. Each year they signed up the same members, along with any newcomers they could interest.

Mrs. Mengel recalls: "It was really something to see Mrs. Fox in action at that time. She always came into headquarters on the Mezza-

3 Ruby Stearns, "Around El Paso," El Paso *Times,* May 30, 1953, p. 11.

nine of the Del Norte, just before closing time on the last day of the drive. Flushed with triumph, she would produce a jumble of signed cards and heaven help anybody who had tried to 'work' one of her names! She rarely had collected the money, which had to be turned in on that very day. So there she would sit, with one of her big hats on, pen in hand, going over her cards and writing check after check to pay for the memberships she was reporting. Workers received free tickets, you know, with a certain number of signed-up members. Goodness knows she did not need the free tickets, but she was a great competitor and she wanted to win. She probably gave them away to students or hard-up musical friends."[4]

4 Interview, July 7, 1972.

CHAPTER XIV

The Era of Elliott

＊ IN THE MID-1940S AN EL PASO MAN entered Josephine's life, a man who was to contribute greatly to the building of her estate and have more direct influence on her, perhaps, than any man since the death of her husband. He was William J. (Bill) Elliott, a widower and the father of four grown children. His sons are Jim and Dave, who with their families reside in El Paso; the daughters are Marilyn Singerman, Dayton, Ohio, and Patricia Ann Turner, Fairbanks, Alaska.

Bill Elliott had come to El Paso in 1939 and had been active in real estate since his arrival. He was a dynamic man of great energy and vision. He realized that a building boom was inevitable at the end of World War II and he envisioned acres of new homes on Josephine's land in the Lower Valley, which was then only cotton fields. He owned a corporation, El Paso Properties, and he proposed to Josephine that they develop subdivisions through the corporation, assisted by Mac Murchison of Mortgage Investment Company. Mrs. Fox may have been hesitant at first, since cotton had been bringing her a fine income, but she caught Bill's enthusiasm and work was begun.

At the suggestion of Mr. Elliott a preliminary study had been made in 1946 by Will Gordon Norris, a planning consultant from Los Angeles, for which Mrs. Fox had paid a fee of $850.00. The entire Clardy-Fox subdivision was covered in the plan. This study was the basis for laying out the land.

A few lots had been sold for homes in 1939 in an area called Clardy Subdivision No. 1, Winchester Cooley acting as agent to secure Federal Housing Administration loans. The development was not continued after the death of Mrs. Clardy in 1940. Now that Bill Elliott was developing the subdivision, it was decided to call the area Clardy-Fox No. 2 and as work progressed, Clardy-Fox No. 3 was to be laid out and developed.

The land which Bill proposed to develop was in the town of Ascarate and he suggested to Mrs. Fox that she arrange to have it taken into the city of El Paso so utilities could be obtained, a change which was readily accomplished. He wrote her a memorandum on April 20, 1949, outlining his plan, detailing the cost per building site for paving, curb, gutter, sewer and water. He was to buy the lots at $400 per site and the "development would go forward in groups of about 50 lots, beginning at Blanco Street and working South on both of the proposed new streets in a contiguous manner with no vacant lots left."

WILLIAM J. (BILL) ELLIOTT

Lance Engineering laid out the first tract of 56.7 acres containing 235 lots. Carrying the calculation to the whole tract, Bill Elliott wrote Josephine there would be 835 home building sites, a school site, space for a shopping center and 20 acres north of the highway to be reserved for a "tourist court." His estimate of what Josephine would realize from all this was well over one million dollars.

This was heady talk to Josephine. With money such as this, she could buy many fine hats and diamond bracelets. She could purchase all the beautiful antiques that her heart desired. "If only little Mama and dear Eugene could have lived to share it with me," she may have thought, as she signed the papers and gave Bill Elliott the go-ahead signal.

Bill Elliott not only handled the development of the Clardy-Fox subdivisions but he soon found that Josephine was asking him to take care of many other business and personal affairs for her. As Josephine freely admitted, she liked men and she liked Bill a great deal. In fact, she is said to have thought of him as a good prospect for marriage, but somehow Bill never regarded their friendship in that light.

Bill and Josephine ate lunch together every day at the same table in the Del Norte Hotel dining room. It was a business conference where many details were handled. Often it would be necessary for Mrs. Fox to confer with others involved in her affairs. Then she would adjourn to the Mezzanine floor of the hotel, where papers could be spread out, maps studied, contracts discussed. After one such session, Mary White Boykin came along and saw Josephine sitting there looking very tired and weary. Josephine said to her long-time friend, "Oh, it seems that I never have time for any fun. I just work all the time." Mrs. Boykin advised her: "Put yourself in the hands of the bank and let them handle your affairs, as I do." But Josephine said she couldn't do that; she must look after her business herself.

When Mary had been a little girl her father, Zach White (who built the Paso del Norte Hotel where Mary and her husband, Col. Jess Boykin, live) built his mansion on North Mesa Avenue. At that time Josephine and her mother lived in a house on North Oregon, just behind the White home. Sometimes Mrs. Clardy would call Mrs. White and say "If Mary wants to see Josephine's new dress, tell her to run over right quick, as she is putting it on now and will be going out soon."

Mary, who was always interested in clothes and fashion, would run over and admire the elegant young lady in all her finery. Then sometimes there would be cookies or some other treat for her which the Chinese cook kept ready in the Clardy kitchen for little girls like herself.

Now many years had passed and Josephine, a widow and an orphan, sometimes seemed rather pathetic to Mary Boykin as she saw her at work during those long business meetings in the hotel.

Josephine Fox was surprised and somewhat disconcerted when Bill Elliott announced in 1957 that he had married Norma Lott Webster. Norma, a former El Pasoan, had been living in Phoenix for two years, having been transferred there by Addressograph, the company for whom she was office manager in El Paso. She and Bill were married in a quiet ceremony on March 15, 1957, in the chapel of the Central Avenue Methodist Church in Phoenix.

"Mrs. Fox seemed to resent me at first and always sort of looked down her nose at me," Norma said, "but eventually we got to be friends." Perhaps Josephine feared she would lose some of the attention and services she had received from Bill, now that he had a wife. It proved, however that she gained more than she lost, for Norma was an unselfish person, completely devoted to Bill and his interests, never seeming to resent the demands on his time made by Mrs. Fox. Instead she added her own talents for thoughtfulness and kindness to the situation.

Norma recalls that she and Bill would go to Josephine's house on New Year's morning to watch the annual Sun Carnival Parade. Norma took coffee and rolls along and acted as hostess when friends dropped in. In earlier years, Josephine told her, she had always attended the parade Open House at the home of her neighbors, Judge and Mrs. Ballard Coldwell.

These parties were always lively, Josephine recalled, what with the Coldwell children and their friends running in and out of the house and the Judge keeping everybody entertained with his amusing comments and stories. Afterward Josephine would sometimes invite a young friend of whom she was quite fond, Miss Margarita Gomez of Juarez, to go home with her for a bit of refreshment. Margarita said, "We would sit and drink champagne and eat a bit of cake, which Mrs. Fox served from a daintily appointed table, using her beautiful linens and silver. She was a very ceremonious person and loved to do things with formality in those days."

By the time Norma Elliott came along, though, most of that formality had been forgotten, it seems. Often there was very little in the house to eat, but Josephine always kept a well-stocked bar, Norma said. "She loved bright lights, people and gaiety and was very pleased when people came in, although only her closest friends were admitted, and she hardly ever thought to provide any food for them. Mundane housekeeping details she seemed to find boresome."

The subdivisions were doing very well under the guiding genius of Bill Elliott, who was assisted by his brothers Ray and Harry. As houses were built and sold, Tom Newman of Pioneer Title Co. and Mac Murchison of Mortgage Investment Co. carried the deals through to completion. Attorney Wyndham White acted as trustee for many of the transactions.

Josephine's fortunes were building steadily, but two more developments were ahead that would really make her a wealthy woman. They were the sale of land for the Clardy-Fox Shopping Center and the sale to the U. S. Government of land for the Paisano Postoffice building. Bill Elliott helped to cosummate both transactions.

Negotiations for the shopping center started in 1955 when Josephine Fox signed a contract with Julius Kaufman of New York City and J. Ted Cottle of El Paso for the sale of twenty-one acres of her land in the Elijah Bennett Survey, Lower Valley. The price was to be something over $400,000.00. A great deal of work was involved in getting the shopping center organized. Merchants had to be signed

Ground-breaking for Fox-Plaza Shopping Center.
J. Francis Morgan, J. Ted Cottle, Mrs. Fox, Julius Kaufman.

up, leases agreed upon, financing arranged, plans for buildings drawn and many other details worked out. Finally, ground was broken in 1958 and the Fox-Plaza Shopping Center had its official opening July 1, 1959. Morgan Brothers, El Paso construction firm, handled the building contract.

On Feb. 8, 1958, Bill Elliott gave an announcement to the El Paso *Times* that the Postoffice Department in Washington had approved the purchase of a tract on Paisano and Cortez Streets belonging to Josephine Clardy Fox for the erection of a new postoffice in El Paso. Consideration for the land was $345,000, which was paid in cash. C. H. Leavell Co. built the facility, total cost of which was just under two million dollars. Groundbreaking was held on May 8, 1961. But Bill Elliott was not present for the occasion. He had died of a heart attack a few days earlier, on April 24.

Many of Bill Elliott's services to Josephine were personal and she would miss him in many areas beside that of the business partnership. She never liked to travel alone and liked to have some one make all the arrangements for her trips before she left El Paso. She called on Bill to help her with this, and then after arrangements were made, he would take her to New York, get her settled, then return home to take care of business affairs.

After Bill and Norma were married, Bill usually would accompany Josephine to New York (her poor eyesight made it difficult for her to travel alone), then when her stay was over, he and Norma would both fly there to bring her home. Mrs. Fox stayed at the St. Regis Hotel in New York.

One year in New York, she met a young Italian singer, Pietro Gentile, who delighted her with his European manners and soon won her friendship. Through Pietro she learned of a beautiful, almost new Cadillac, 1957 model, which a doctor friend of his wanted to sell. It was an Eldorado Broughham, with many luxury features and very low mileage, one of only 200 such models made that year by the company. Josephine fell in love with the car and bought it, paying about $13,000 for the car, which had a list price of $18,000. It seemed that Pietro had hoped to drive Josephine to El Paso in the car, but when she had it shipped and flew home, he came along to teach her how to drive it. Soon after they arrived in El Paso, he proposed that they drive to California and Josephine agreed. In July, 1958, they left El

Paso on an ill-fated trip. Pietro drove off the road in Arizona dragging the underpart of the low-slung Cadillac. In vain he tried to summon aid, but no one would stop to help them, so he decided to drive on into Phoenix, which he did although the motor was heating badly. When they reached a garage, they found that the motor was burned up and a complete new one would have to be ordered from the factory, and other extensive repairs made. They left the car there, rented another and drove to Las Vegas, Nevada for a short holiday, flying back to El Paso after a few days.

When the Cadillac was finally repaired, months later, as Norma recalls, she and Bill Elliott flew to Phoenix and drove it back to El Paso.

PIETRO GENTILE

Needless to say, when Mrs. Fox called on Bill to fly with her to New York, or for other extraordinary duties, she paid all expenses. Her business conferences sometimes ran on for hours, detaining Bill from his own business interests and he found it hard to be patient at times. Another real estate agent, James E. Rogers, who handled property and insurance for Mrs. Fox, says that she paid Bill a retainer, but his brother Ray says he never heard of it if she did. "Bill made lots of money," Ray said, "but he was a big spender so he never kept much of it."

Bill went on to develop other subdivisions in association with other landowners, so his influence on the face of El Paso, especially on the West Side of the city, was great.

CHAPTER XV

Of Counts, Cabbages and Collections

◄§ IN JANUARY OF 1957, A DEALER IN ART named Count Ivan Podgoursky came to El Paso to present an exhibit at the Public Library and, at a reception which opened the show, was introduced to prominent citizens and art collectors by Mrs. J. C. (Louise) Wilmarth, member of the library board, Miss Elizabeth Kelly, librarian, and others connected with the library.[1] During the exhibit, the Count displayed extensive charm, elegant manners, and a way of ingratiating himself with the ladies. All of his continental polish was brought into play when he met Josephine Clardy Fox, who became his chief client in El Paso.

Count Ivan Podgoursky[2] came to El Paso well recommended as an art connoisseur, a reputation which was enhanced by a beautiful catalogue issued by the Little Rock Museum of Fine Arts on the occasion of an exhibit there of paintings loaned by Podgoursky. William E. Steadman, Jr., director of the museum, wrote in a foreword, "Count Podgoursky is a discriminating collector. His taste and knowledge have combined to assemble a group of paintings of the highest artistic merit, making this one of the outstanding collections of its kind in

[1] Louise Maxon, "Reception Opens Show of European Masters," *The El Paso Times,* January 27, 1957, p. 10.

[2] Arriving in Texas from Boston about 1951, Count Ivan Podgoursky settled in San Antonio where he became established as an art dealer. His first wife had been a beautiful young Boston socialite, who had died tragically in an automobile accident. Shortly after coming to San Antonio, the Count was separated from his second wife, Bianca of Falmouth, Massachusetts, and he obtained an annulment of their twelve-year marriage on the grounds that Bianca had falsely claimed to be of noble birth. In his testimony during the annulment proceedings, Podgoursky told the judge that he was a White Russian of noble lineage who had fled the Bolskeviks as a young man after having served as a cavalry lieutenant in the Czar's army. "I am not a wealthy man, only moderately well to do," he said. "What money I have made is from buying and selling art in the United States. None of it came from Russia." In 1960, Ivan married Mary Babicki, who had been his housekeeper in San Antonio for several years.

this country." Steadman was proud of his role in persuading Count Podgoursky to bring together the superb collection of paintings, which was made up mainly of the work of French artists of the Nineteenth Century.

The collection included other works, one of which was listed as item 27 in the catalogue, a painting titled "Aurora" by Tom Lea of El Paso. The account of how Podgoursky came into possession of this painting has been told by Mr. Lea himself.

Ivan was at a small party in my home when he saw my painting of a nude which I called 'Aurora.' He and all of us had partaken of a few libations during the evening, after which Ivan persisted in asking me to sell him the picture. I said it was not for sale, but when Podgoursky got too much to drink he could become rather loud and obnoxious. So I finally said I would not sell the painting but would give it to him if he would take it and get out, which he did.

The next morning Ivan must have realized that he had not behaved properly at my party. He called up and was very apologetic, wanted to pay me for the picture and declared that I was his best friend and he did not want to offend me. He must pay me in some way for the wonderful painting. So I said all right, my wife wanted a Rembrandt print and if he could find one, that would be acceptable as payment. To my surprise, he came up with the Rembrandt print, a very good one at that, and everybody was happy.

I remember that when Ivan came to town, he would invite Sarah and me, the Dan Ponders and the Charles Leavells to dinner in Juarez. One evening he had taken us to dinner at the Fiesta over there, and we three men insisted that we would buy the wine for the dinner, which he was to select. He went into a lengthy conference with the head waiter and we had excellent wine, selected especially for each course. It really must have been fine stuff, for when we got ready to pay for it, we were astounded to learn that such expensive vintages exist — the wine for the seven of us cost almost $200! [3]

During the years after Josephine met Count Podgoursky from 1957 to his death in 1962, she bought a large number of paintings and a few art objects, including the "Easter Egg by Faberge" which were offered her either by Podgoursky himself or by Count Louis Von Cseh, another art dealer whom Podgoursky introduced to her. The two men originally operated together to sell art and art objects to clients, but eventually they came to a parting of the way. In fact, Podgour-

[3] Interview, Tom Lea, February, 1973.

sky and Von Cseh became involved in a bitter lawsuit in 1961 over ownership of certain paintings and commissions on sales of paintings to Josephine Fox. Ivan asserted in the legal brief[4] of the counter-suit which he filed in U. S. District Court in Houston that in July of 1959 "as is usual and customary in the business of art brokerage" he entered into an agreement and contract with Louis Von Cseh that he would at his own expense introduce Von Cseh to certain of his established clients and that they would share on a fifty-fifty basis the profits on any sales made by Von Cseh to these clients, or if the cost could not be established Ivan was to receive not less than one-third of the selling price. They entered into a definite agreement that any future sales to Mrs. Eugene (Josephine) Fox would be governed by this contract.

Thereupon Ivan took Von Cseh with him to El Paso and introduced him to Mrs. Fox and other established clients. During this trip (the brief asserts) they sold Mrs. Fox a jeweled flower for which Von Cseh paid Ivan $1100 as his share of the profit. They also presented some paintings and other art objects. As they had been unable to sell the painting titled "Adoration of the Magi," attributed to Van Dyke, Ivan agreed to build up the importance, standing and value of the painting, the validity of which was questioned, and he was proceeding to do this when the "disputes, breach of contract, and tortuous conduct on the part of the cross-defendant [Von Cseh] caused the cross-plaintiff [Podgoursky] to cease such efforts."[5]

Ivan alleged in the brief that he was notified in 1960 that Von Cseh had breached the contract by making sales to his client, Mrs. Josephine Fox, without notice to him or tendering the agreed commission. He lists eight paintings and two art objects (including the "Jeweled Easter Egg" by Carl Faberge) upon which he was due an accounting, saying that his commission on these items should "substantially exceed $85,000."[6]

For further cause of action (the brief stated) Ivan claimed he had built up a reputation for fair dealing, respectability and integrity and

4 Information regarding this suit is recorded in Civil Action No. 13,453, United States District Court for the Southern District of Texas, Houston Division. Irene Von Cseh and husband, Louis Von Cseh, Plaintiffs v. Roland De France and Ivan Podgoursky, Defendants. See also the First Amended Answer and Counter Claim of Defendant, Ivan Podgoursky.

5 Ibid.   6 Ibid.

that Von Cseh "has maliciously and without justification libeled my ownership to three paintings submitted for sale to Mr. Reginald Fisher, curator El Paso Museum of Art." He listed the paintings as *Still Life,* attributed to Zurbaran and offered at $12,000; *Portrait of George Washington,* by Gilbert Stuart and offered at $35,000; *Birth of Christ,* by Murillo and offered at $17,500.

Podgoursky claimed that his ownership was libeled by a telegram which Von Cseh had sent to Dr. Reginald Fisher: PLEASE HOLD STILL LIFE AND ALL OTHER PAINTINGS LEFT WITH YOU BY IVAN PODGOURSKY UNTIL FURTHER LEGAL NOTIFICATION. PICTURES ARE MY PROPERTY GIVEN TO PODGOURSKY ON CONSIGNMENT — LOUIS VON CSEH.[7]

He states that in addition to such libel the cross-defendant by telephone slandered the name and reputation of cross-plaintiff (Podgoursky) by telling his clients in El Paso that he was "unreliable, untrustworthy, dishonest and disreputable." Ivan asked for exemplary damages of $100,000 and for judgment against the cross-defendants in the sum of $252,500.[8] The suit was settled out of court after Podgoursky's death and it would be difficult to determine who won.

In an inventory[9] of Josephine's paintings drawn up for insurance in March, 1963, the following items were listed:

Faberge Easter Egg, $25,000; "Amusement Champetre" — Watteau, $45,000; "Bust Portrait of a Young Woman" — Rubens, $50,000; "Gypsy Girl" — Hoppner, $30,000; "The Angler" — Boucher, $30,000; "Fine Summer's Day" — Hobbema, $40,000; "Portrait of Young Gentlemen" — Gainesborough, $20,000; "Madonna With Clasped Hands" — Sassaferato, $20,000; "Madame Boucher" — Boucher, $78,000; "King Charles I" — Velasquez, $10,000; "Mme. de Clairon" — Fraganeur, $20,000; "Portrait of G. Washington" — Stuart, $35,000; "Birth of Christ" — Murillo, $20,000; "Guitar Player" — Watteau, $65,000; "Castel Gondolfo" — Corot, $12,500.

These valuations were based on authentications furnished Mrs. Fox, although it is unlikely she paid these prices. It is the practice of some art dealers to furnish expertise (or authentication) with estimated value of a painting much higher than the price at which he offers it to the client, thus holding out the prospect that the painting can be sold later at a profit.

It is a sad commentary on the wide gulf between these valuations and the prices listed by Parke-Bernet experts when they appraised

7 Ibid.   8 Ibid.   9 A copy is in the U.T. El Paso Archives.

the Fox estate after Josephine's death. The only painting appraised close to the above figure is the Corot "Castel Gondolfo," at $10,000. The Washington portrait was labeled "after Gilbert Stuart," giving it a price tag of $4,000. (Since Stuart is said to have painted one hundred portraits of Washington, all done from the same sitting, it is thought this may be one of Stuart's own copies." When Stuart was once asked why he did not sign his works, he replied, "I mark them all over.")[10] A *Still Life*, Dutch School of the early Seventeenth Century, was appraised by Parke-Bernet at $3,000. All others were given valuations of a few hundred dollars. Mrs. Fox did acquire the disputed painting *Adoration of the Magi* which Parke-Bernet labeled "Spanish School, 18th Century" and gave a valuation of $600.

As for the "Faberge Easter Egg" which Josephine had listed at $25,000 and which she believed to be the genuine work of the famous Russian court jeweler, the experts from Parke-Bernet gave it a value of only $350. She also had in her possession several of the jeweled flowers set in rock crystal bases in the style of the master and all stamped Faberge. If they were genuine, they too, would have a value running into five figures, but alas, they are also appraised as copies; one was valued at $125, the others at $150 each.

In April 1962, Count Podgoursky was bludgeoned to death by his stepson, Vladimir Podgoursky, 23, who was a Trinity University student at the time. Vladimir said he returned home to find a fierce argument raging between Ivan and Mary, his wife (the boy's mother) and that he intervened because the Count was abusing his mother; whereupon the Count seized a butcher knife and chased him through several rooms of the house. In self-defense, he said, Vladimir picked up a heavy bronze bookend and struck his step-father on the head. He was arrested and charged with murder but was no-billed by the Grand Jury when the case came up a few months later, and then was freed. The Count was sixty-one at the time of his death and his wife was forty-three.

Vladimir, whose real name was William Lapko, was the next eldest of his mother's three sons by previous marriages. He and the youngest, age ten, were living in the Podgoursky home. He had taken the Podgoursky name because the Count was in the process of adopting

10 Fort Wayne *News-Sentinel*, May 17, 1952: article by art critic Bertha Stein Duemling.

him and was using him as a secretary and chauffeur and wanted the boy identified as a son for business reasons.

Newspaper accounts said the Podgoursky home was worth $150,-000 and that every room was piled full of paintings and valuable art objects. The temporary administrator, Frank Baskin, estimated the worth of the paintings at $300,000. Mary Podgoursky stated right after the Count's death that she was penniless; that her husband owed on the house and had many other debts. "I could not keep the house, even if it were paid for," she said, "because the upkeep is tremendous." [11]

The bulk of the estate was left to her, but the will was contested by the "so-called second wife," according to a letter which Vladimir wrote to Josephine. That and many other court battles had to be fought by Mary Podgoursky, who was named administrator in the will. Vladimir acted as agent for the estate and appeared to be very knowledgeable about the art dealer's affairs and methods of doing business.

Josephine had made only partial payment for several paintings and probably had one or two others under consideration when the Count died. Vladimir acknowledged receipt of her checks and discussed paintings in several lengthy letters written during the next two or three years. One of the paintings for which Josephine owed the Count was *Castel Gondolfo* and upon forwarding a check in the amount of $2,500 she received a receipt from Vladimir saying it represented complete payment. He enclosed a legal bill of sale for the painting signed by his mother. He wrote:

I have also enclosed two photographs of your Spanish *Still Life* painting as well as one of your lovely portrait by Marquise de Belfons and one of your beautiful Pater. The third affidavit for the Watteau painting 'The Guitar Player' arrived today and I have forwarded it to your attorney, Mr. Smith. I believe this now fulfills all your requirements on the sale of this painting on which a $2,000 balance remains.

He sent a lengthy explanation of the Russian Icon of the Virgin "with three hands," saying that a man who had his hand healed donated a hand made of gold in the form and size of the Virgin's hand and that it was permanently attached to the original icon. This third hand was copied by icon painters from the Fourteenth Century as a

[11] San Antonio *Express, Light and News*, April 22, 1962 to May 29, 1964.

characteristic feature of the miraculous icon. "These miraculous three-handed icons of Our Lady, such as the 19th Century Russian one you have, are very rare, especially in the United States, and are much sought-after objects," he wrote Josephine.

This letter was written to Josephine in March, 1964, and Vladimir said he and his mother had hoped to visit her before the eye operation to give her all the encouragement they could, but had been prevented from doing so. Now that they had received good news about the success of the surgery, they were very happy. "Please give our thanks to Mrs. Branch and Mr. Moreno for their kindness in keeping us informed about the matter."

During 1963 and 1964 Josephine received several letters from Count Von Cseh, who was still selling art objects to her. She had full knowledge about the court action and his disputes with Podgoursky but her relationship to him seemed as friendly as ever. On August 29, 1963 he wrote:

I received your letter and cashier's check. Thank you for sending it. Enclosed are some pages from my manuscript. I hope you enjoy reading it. If you do, I will most certainly send you more. A list of four paintings followed with valuations and selling prices and a fifth item, a "17th Century Jeweled cabinet with clock, a true masterpiece: $8,000." He said she had asked for this information and closed by saying "I wish I could be with you — I so enjoy our little visits. . . . Take care of yourself. With love, C. Louis.

In addition to paintings and antique furniture, Josephine loved and collected many other things such as beautiful and historic fans, rare and valuable boxes ranging in size from miniature to large examples of the silversmith's art, porcelains from all parts of the world and clocks of all descriptions. From her clock collection a beautiful garniture (Sevres clock and matching candlesticks) was transferred to the reception room of Hoover House, the pieces dating to 1780. Other items at Hoover House included a pair of unusual oak vitrines in Louis XVI style holding a collection of fine Limoges enamels and a small Roza oil painting in a gilt frame; also a French Trumeau mirror above an Adam commode, a small Limoges and crystal lamp, and several pieces from her collection of fine cut glass.

In the entry hall of Hoover House on either side of the front doorway were placed two large Sevres urns, signed and dated 1771, on matching gilt pedestals with rose Carrara marble tops. In the center of this spacious entry an oval table in Louis V style was placed and hung on the wall of the stairway were several landscapes from the Fox collection. Near the steps leading to a lower level doorway, a copy of a Raphael madonna in an elaborate oval gilt frame was hung. In the dining room many of the paintings, a pair of French screens, a tall silver epergne, a George III silver tea service, and a rare pair of Peruvian silver candlesticks were used.[12]

Beautiful cabinets holding examples of Meissen and Sevres from the Fox collection have been placed in the office of the president of UT El Paso and in the executive suite on campus. The portrait of Washington, a French enamel clock and candelabra, along with a fine rug of Josephine's, are also to be seen on campus. Several French cabinets and an unusual Chinese one were placed in the University library, where they are used as current displays. The Fox collection of about one thousand books went to the library, including some very old and rare books. Dale Walker, writing in *Nova*, reported:

Examining the old books, UT El Paso librarians made a very important discovery: in riffling the pages or bending slightly the entire inside contents of certain of the old books, the gilt of the fore-edge (that is, the right-hand open edge of the book as opposed to the back edge or spine, along which the book is stitched and bound,) disappears and in its place, startlingly, a picture becomes visible.

It was discovered that 13 of Mrs. Fox's books contain these mysterious pictures.

When the books were called to the attention of the University Librarian Baxter Polk, he recognized them instantly as rare fore-edge paintings, having seen examples of them in years past.[13]

A small gallery in the Centennial Museum on campus was filled with the Fox antique furniture, including large cabinets holding rare and valuable vases and art objects. At one end of the room, the R. Hinton Perry life-size paintings of lovely young Josephine in her blue gown surveys the scene with serenity.[14] In the vaults, many of her valuables were placed, such as Georgian silver pieces and a marvelous silver flatware service for twelve crafted by Faberge for the household of the Russian Czar. Probably no other museum in the world can match this rare treasure.

[12] This description of items in Hoover House made June 30, 1972.
[13] Dale Walker, "Art Beneath the Gilt," *Nova* V (Summer, 1970), p. 8.

An amusing story is told by Florence Cathcart Melby about some fine silver pieces brought out of Germany soon after the war that found their way into the El Paso shop of Mrs. J. P. McGrath. Florence says she happened to be in the shop when some German scientists from New Mexico brought the pieces in. She immediately fell in love with an ornate silver box, a sort of jewel casket having cherubs atop the lid. She bought it and some silver trays. Later Mrs. Fox heard about the silver and bought a dozen silver service plates. Sometime afterward she and her good friend, Dr. Lucinda Templin, principal of Radford School for Girls, were having afternoon tea at the Melby home and spied the silver box. "Josephine, you should have that box for your collection," Lucinda said. Mrs. Fox agreed and asked Florence if she would consider selling it. "Many times in the past, I had let Josephine talk me out of beautiful things which we both wanted for our collections," Florence said, "but this time I decided that I couldn't let her have the box, so I held my ground and kept it." Mrs. Fox and Mrs. Melby both bought some of the lovely things offered in the estate sale after the death of Mrs. A. P. Coles. Mrs. Fox also acquired some of her treasures from Mrs. Otto Nordwald, who had brought them out of Mexico. Mrs. Nordwald and Mrs. Fox became close friends, drawn together by their love of beautiful things, says Mrs. Ruth Howell, daughter of the late Mrs. Nordwald.

The El Paso dealers from whom Josephine acquired many precious items for her collection were John and Rena Gillett, who had their home and antique shop near her on Montana Street for many years. After they moved to Laguna Beach, California, several years ago, they still bought things for Josephine, corresponded with her regularly and they came to El Paso to see her from time to time. In a letter John says that she was a dear friend and neighbor with whom they felt kinship because of her love of beautiful things. "One time when she was ill at home, we prepared and took her dinner to her every evening for about a month. Once she asked us what we would like for her to leave us in her will. We replied 'just your love and affection.'" The valuable Faberge flatware table service was obtained for Josephine by the Gilletts. They also sold her fine crystal and porcelains.

Josephine bought some fine porcelains from Mr. and Mrs. Bernard F. Heiler in 1963-64 when they were planning to move away from El

14 See frontispiece, page vi.

Paso. Mrs. Heiler says they had traveled all over the world collecting these beautiful and rare pieces, during her husband's work for the United States State Department.

Another dealer in antiques and art, B. F. Cass of Dallas, supplied Mrs. Fox with oriental rugs and art objects in her collection. He had cousins in El Paso and used to come here in a van, bringing fine things that might be of interest to Mrs. Fox and other clients.

Byron Merkin, of the Popular Dry Goods Co. was a dear friend of Mrs. Fox and he frequently ordered art objects and did many favors for her. He is one of the few El Pasoans who visited often in her home, sometimes summoned there to share her joy when she had acquired something of beauty which she felt he would find pleasure in seeing. Among El Paso jewelers who had entree to the Fox home and who sold her fine things were Nate Feder, Geof Holdsworth and John Rogers.

Two other friends who assisted Josephine in finding additions to her collections were Frances Vance (now Mrs. Serene Durling) and Dr. Lucinda Templin. When it came to advising Josephine about insurance of her fine things, James E. Rogers and his daughter, Miss Betty Rogers were consulted. Betty made innumerable lists of all the paintings, the silver, and the jewelry. When Josephine was in the hospital for long periods, she would summon Betty, perhaps just because she was lonely, and ask her to make a new list of some collection, or to go to the Fox home and check on valuables. For security reasons during her illness, it was decided that all locks on the Fox home should be changed, therefore, double locks were installed. This meant that two persons, each carrying a key, had to go together to enter the house. Betty and Mrs. Branch, a nurse, each had a set of such keys and went together to the house on errands for Mrs. Fox during the last few years of her life.

CHAPTER XVI

Fall and Decline

✑ᔥ JOSEPHINE WAS IN DALLAS in 1959 for the Neiman-Marcus Fall Fortnight, an annual festival of gaiety, bright lights, spectacular displays and fashionable parties. Celebrities and socialites came from near and far to be guests at the affair. Mrs. Fox, a customer of the store, was well known there, especially in the department of gifts and antiques where Carl Wright[1] was the buyer. On Josephine's trips to Dallas, through the years, she and Carl had become friends and he would often escort her to the opera or to a concert or movie. "She had a great sense of humor and I enjoyed her company," he said. "I sensed that she was really a very lonely person and I tried to see that she was entertained while here." He recalled one evening when they were to attend the opera and he was waiting for her in the lobby of her hotel. "She came down wearing her diamonds, an elegant white sequin gown, and swirls of white net about her shoulders, setting off her jet black hair. She really made quite a picture, and just as she arrived, Mr. Stanley Marcus and several members of his family came along. I introduced Mrs. Fox and we chatted together for a few minutes." After that, Josephine took pride in mentioning to friends that she knew the owner of Neiman-Marcus personally.

"Mrs. Fox and I were at the opera together on the evening when Maria Callas gave her famous fiery performance of *Medea*," Carl recalls. "Callas had just been dismissed from the Met that day and she was in a rage. I never heard such singing nor saw such acting. It was an evening never to be forgotten," he said.

Bill and Norma Elliott had accompanied Josephine to Dallas for the 1959 Fortnight. In the late twilight of a pleasant September Sunday, they all returned to the Statler-Hilton Hotel after an afternoon spent

[1] He now has his own shop in Dallas, filled with treasures which he has collected by roaming the world. In speaking of the beautiful art objects he sold Josephine, he says some are almost priceless now, especially the genuine old Limoges enamels.

with Carl Wright, viewing Neiman-Marcus exhibits. They were to see Carl again the next day.

As they went up to their rooms Josephine suggested, "Let's have dinner here in the hotel tonight, if it suits you. Shall we meet in the dining room in an hour?" The Elliotts agreed. During dinner the three El Pasoans talked over events of the day and discussed plans for the next day. Afterward, as they were leaving the dining room, Mrs. Fox missed her footing on a low step leading to the lobby, fell heavily and sustained a broken hip. Bill and Norma knew at once that she was badly hurt. The hotel doctor was called, an ambulance was sent for, and Josephine was taken to St. Paul's Hospital.

By the time Josephine was settled in her room and Bill had handled matters with the business office, it was after midnight when he and Norma were able to return to the hotel. The doctors had told them that the broken hip could not be set for a few days and advised that they get Mrs. Fox back to El Paso and under the care of her own doctors as soon as possible. There was a morning train, so the Elliotts started arrangements to get her on it.

Fortunately Bill Elliott had seen Sam Young of El Paso in the hotel that afternoon. Mr. Young, president of El Paso National Bank, went into action immediately when Bill called to tell him of the accident. Messages were sent to doctors and friends in El Paso while Mr. Young contacted officials of the Texas and Pacific Railroad to ask that a pullman car on the morning train be set on a siding where Mrs. Fox could be transferred from an ambulance into a berth, and reserving space for the Elliotts to accompany her to El Paso.

Very early that morning Bill went to the hospital, where he settled accounts and helped to get Josephine into the ambulance. She had spent a restless night despite sedation, and was in great pain. Bill rode in the ambulance with her to the railroad siding where the pullman was waiting. Windows had been removed so that the stretcher could be lifted into the car.

Norma was there, along with Carl Wright, who had brought her and the luggage in his own car from the hotel. It was a somber occasion, in contrast to the happy afternoon they had spent together on Sunday. The train pulled out and thus began the long, painful journey which ended about eighteen hours later when they arrived in El Paso near midnight on September 14, 1959.

Norma Elliott stood over Josephine throughout that long day, trying to care for the anguished woman constantly writhing in pain. Although the railroad people were as helpful as possible, little could be done, for there were no facilities available. "I felt very helpless," Norma said, "I had nothing with which to alleviate her pain as she could not tolerate or retain drugs, not even aspirin. She was nauseated, still in shock, groaning and crying out at every bump or lurch of the train. I thought we would never reach El Paso; it was the most difficult ordeal I have ever known."

When they did arrive in El Paso, a little group was waiting on the platform to assist in taking Mrs. Fox to the hospital. Included were her physician, Dr. Lester Feener, her close friend, Mrs. Frances Vance Durling, Joe Moreno, and Gus Bianche. Mrs. Durling and Dr. Feener rode in the ambulance with Josephine to Providence Memorial Hospital, where arrangements had been made for her admittance. An exhausted Bill and Norma Elliott, who had not slept for almost forty-eight hours, took a cab home. Among Josephine's possessions which they carried with them was a satin case filled with valuable jewelry. "We didn't dare let that case get out of our sight during the whole trip from Dallas," Norma said.

As soon as Mrs. Fox was able to undergo surgery, the hip was set and a pin inserted, the procedure performed by Dr. Morton Leonard, an orthopedic surgeon. She was to spend the next fourteen months recuperating in Providence Memorial Hospital. Friends said that Josephine sometimes chafed at the strict orders of Dr. Leonard, but she must have enjoyed his visits. He was young and handsome as well as skilled, also a fine musician with a beautiful baritone voice with whom she could talk about music and opera.

Josephine must have been very happy when, at the end of the following year the doctors decided she was well enough to leave the hospital and go home for Christmas. She left Providence on December 5, 1960, taking her faithful nurses, Mrs. Katherine Crites and Mrs. Margaret Branch, with her.

On May 8, 1961, Mrs. Fox attended the groundbreaking for the new postal facility on Paisano Drive and was introduced as former owner of the site. Dignitaries present included representatives of the Post-office Department from Washington and El Paso, as well as city and

The Clardy Fox Room
Centennial Museum — The University of Texas at El Paso

In the Clardy Fox room of the Centennial Museum: The inlaid vitrine with mantle garniture is in Louis XV style; the marble bust, porcelain center table, and velvet painting are Victorian. In the background is a Chinese black lacquer cabinet.

18th and 19th century Sevres and Dresden porcelain objects. The blue and gold porcelain urn with clock was one of Mrs. Fox's favorites.

Five of the 72 folding fans from the Clardy Fox collection. The painted figures and delicate lace work indicate French origins of 18th and 19th centuries.

These art objects are in the style of Carl Faberge, master jeweler to the Russian court in the last century.

Cabinet with objets d'art from the Fox collection now in the Executive Suite of the University.

Jacobean style hand-carved oak bookcase cabinet with figurines and urns.

Mahogany and ormolu vitrine with Vernis Martin panels.

Paintings and other rare pieces of furniture enhance the President's office as well as the Hoover House.

county officials. She received a letter on May 10 from El Paso Post-master Charles T. Boyce thanking her for being present.

Another event in 1961 caused Mrs. Fox to receive notice in the El Paso daily newspapers. She gave ground on Lisbon Street for a branch library called the Josephine Clardy Fox Branch of El Paso Public Library, which had its formal opening on November 1. However, it had already seen use before the opening. During August, the bookmobile, which had been going to the area every Saturday, broke down and couldn't make the trip. Miss Elizabeth Kelly, librarian and some assistants, loaded up some books and a card table in a truck and went to the construction site. They made more tables out of saw horses and started circulating books from the front porch.[2]

In 1961 Mrs. Fox gave the final portion of her ownership in a painting *Harlequin and Columbine* by Pater, to the city for El Paso Museum of Art. She had bought the painting from Count Podgoursky for the sum of $20,000. For tax purposes, she gave the painting to the city in three (possibly four) annual installments.

While she was recuperating, Josephine felt rather bitter about her broken hip and all the suffering she had endured. She decided that the least the Hilton Hotel could do would be to compensate her for it. On September 9, 1961, she filed suit in Forty-First District Court of El Paso against the Hilton Hotels Corporation for $565,657. Richard H. Feuille was her attorney, while Thornton Hardie represented the defendant. Mrs. Fox said she had spent $65,657 during her 14-1/2 months in the hospital, for hospital, surgical and medical services and expected to spend $1,500 per month for special care in the future for a long period of time.[3]

There appeared to be little or no evidence of negligence on the part of the hotel management, Mr. Feuille said; and when the defendants asked for a change of venue to a Dallas court, Mrs. Fox decided to compromise and the suit was settled out of court for a nominal sum. Again her friend Sam Young came to her aid, and it was through his good graces that a settlement was reached. Possibly he talked with Conrad Hilton, Sr., himself, who has been for many years a director of El Paso National Bank.

[2] El Paso *Herald-Post*, Aug. 8, 1961.
[3] El Paso *Herald-Post*, Aug. 8, 1961.

During the period of some three years' recuperation at home, Josephine had limited mobility, but did go out occasionally, driven by Mrs. Margaret Branch in the Branch automobile, or by Antonio Ramirez, or by friends. Antonio, who had been in her employ for several years, lived in a small structure known as the Carriage House at the rear of the Fox home. An elevator which Josephine had installed in her home in 1951 proved invaluable now, for it enabled her to go from her upstairs bedroom and sitting room to the lower floor with ease.

The sight in her good eye was becoming dim and an examination showed a developing cataract. Before it was ready for surgery, Josephine became almost blind and was very dependent on her nurses. In 1963, she accepted an invitation to eat Thanksgiving dinner as guest of Woodruff Lochausen in his beautiful small home on the family farm in the upper valley near Anthony, N. M. Woody, a talented pianist and gourmet cook, was following the custom of his older sister, Eda Kimbrough, who before her death often entertained Josie on special occasions in her big house on the farm. Now Woody and a younger sister, Mildred Lochausen Myles, and her husband Ernest Myles drew Josephine into their circle of friends and included her when they entertained at Thanksgiving, Christmas or birthday dinners.

Mrs. Branch drove Josephine to Woody's home and was seated beside her at the festive dinner table. The host and other friends were distressed to note that Josie could not see the food on her plate and had to be helped in eating. The cataract was developing; in a few months she would be completely blind.

She entered Providence Hospital in February where the eye cataract surgery was performed by Dr. Stephen A. Schuster. The results were completely successful and Josie left the hospital in March, 1964 with good vision. Again Mrs. Branch and Mrs. Crites were with her.

Just a few days before Christmas in 1964, Josephine fell in her bedroom at home and broke her bad hip again. Her nurses were downstairs, one just arriving and the other preparing to go off duty. Hearing a thud, they rushed upstairs to find her on the floor in great pain. She was readmitted to Providence where she was to live out the rest of her days.

While she was in the hospital, Mrs. Fox surrounded herself with some of her favorite things. She kept a hat or two on hand to wear when the nurses took her out in a wheel chair for sunning on the terrace, or for rare sorties out of the hospital. Her jewelry also was kept near her, and a few of her favorite paintings were brought from home and hung on the walls of her hospital suite. When she tired of them, they were sent back to her house and others brought in for her enjoyment.

Josephine had a dear friend in Juarez, Roberto Moran, who was owner-manager of La Nueva Cucaracha, a dinner theatre, where she had enjoyed going before her injury. After she had recuperated somewhat, she got permission from her doctor to go there again from time to time to see Roberto, to have dinner and enjoy the floor show. Clothing would be brought from home, the nurses would help her to dress, Josephine would put on her diamonds, and an ambulance would be called to take her to Juarez. On arriving at the doorway of the upstairs nightclub, attendants would put her in a wheel chair and carry her carefully up the steps.

Joe Moreno, vice president of El Paso National Bank, who had helped her with banking matters for years before her injury, now came to the hospital several times each week to help her with her finances. He and Josephine enjoyed a friendly relationship and the nurses told him that even on days when Mrs. Fox was feeling bad, perhaps lethargic, she would brighten up and "come alive" when told "Mr. Moreno is here." Sometimes they would have lunch together at her bedside and Josie would eat better than usual when he was there. She kept wine in her room and would invite him to join her in a little glass. When she conceived the idea of going from the hospital to La Nueva Cucaracha, she asked Joe if he and his wife would be her guests for dinner there, to which they agreed. During the early days of her hospital confinement, the Morenos and the Bill Elliotts alternated in taking Josephine to these dinners in Juarez. After Bill's untimely death, the Morenos were her regular companions on these excursions. "If the show was very good and Mrs. Fox felt well, she would even stay for the late floor show at times," Mr. Moreno said. The shows often were very good indeed, featuring such performers as Carmen Caballero, Guy Lombardo, the Magic Violins and other top entertainers of that day. During the evening, Roberto would stop by the table and chat with Josephine for a while. At these times the invalid seemed able to forget her pain and troubles. Those evenings away from the hospital spent in a setting of lights, good food and drink, among people who were gay and happy, did Josephine more good than medicine, her friends believed. Indeed those trips to La Cucaracha were the best therapy in the world.

The friendship between Josephine and Roberto dated back several years before her accident. Mr. Moreno recalls that he and his wife took Mrs. Fox to the Juarez nightclub for dinner every now and then prior to 1959. She would call and ask them to be her guests for *copitas* at her home, then they would drive her over to La Cucaracha. On one occasion Mrs. Fox called and asked them to come to a "little dinner for Roberto." They had cocktails in her home, then went for dinner at Desert Hills, an El Paso motel. But usually when she saw Roberto it was at his club in Juarez.

In February 1959 Josephine planned a trip to Mexico City to see the new and interesting sights of this "Paris of the West." It was also to be a sentimental journey to revisit scenes she and her mother had known years before. Knowing that Roberto had business interests that took him to Mexico City often, she asked if he would accompany her there to be her interpreter and guide. A date was set and she called on her good friend, Joe Moreno, to help with arrangements. He bought the tickets and helped with her passport. "You know she never told anybody her age," he recalled with a smile," so she wanted me to arrange with the consul to have it state 'Over 21.' I asked Consul General Enrique Ballesteros, a friend and obliging gentleman, who gave his consent. One incident started her trip off badly; somebody stole the money from her purse after she arrived at the Juarez airport. Fortunately, there was time enough to get more cash to her and off she went, excited and happy as a child starting an adventurous journey."

Josephine Clardy Fox died on May 11, 1970. She would have reached her 89th birthday on August 13 that year. She received the final rites of the Roman Catholic Church shortly before death. Mrs. Branch, herself a Catholic, called the priest. She said Mrs. Fox had entreated her: "Do not let me go without the last rites." Since she had no relatives, funeral arrangements were made by Mrs. Branch, Mrs. Crites and Mr. Moreno.

The funeral mass was celebrated by the Rev. John Finnegan in St. Patrick's Cathedral on May 15. It was a cold, windy day, friends said, and only a handful of mourners went to the church and to Evergreen

Cemetery where Josephine was laid to rest beside Eugene and her parents.

Pallbearers were James E. Rogers, Joe M. Moreno, Pearson Wosika, Bruce Bixler, Gus Bianche and Sam D. Young Jr., active; Dr. Lester C. Feener, Dorrance D. Roderick, Sam D. Young Sr., Dr. W. Compere Basom, Dr. Morton Leonard, James A. Keller, Orlando Barera, Hal M. Daugherty, Serene Durling, Herbert Schwartz, Byron Merkin, Ernest Myles, Woodruff Lochausen, Eugene Smith, Freeman Harris, Arthur Gale, the Rev. Glenn Bixler and Dr. Paul N. Poling, honorary.[4]

Mrs. Fox had been active in musical and artistic organizations and in community affairs. She was a director and life member of the El Paso Museum of Arts; a director and member of the Artist Selection committee of El Paso Symphony Orchestra; director and member of Artists committee of Dallas Civic Opera; director and member of nominating and artist committees of El Paso Community Concert Association; a life member of National Society of Arts and Letters; a trustee and life member of El Paso Historical Society; life member of the Texas Western College and the Providence Hospital Auxiliaries; director of National Arts Foundation; member of Pan American Round Table, Woman's Department, Chamber of Commerce; Woman's Club of El Paso, Comadres Club, Knife and Fork Club and El Paso Humane Society. She was a member of the Home Builders Association and the El Paso Board of Realtors.

Because of her gifts to the community, her subdivisions and shopping center, the name of Josephine Clardy Fox was widely known in El Paso. But to most she was just a name, few knew her well. Of those who knew her as a friend many have already been named. Others whose names belong in the list are Orlando Barera, the brilliant conductor of El Paso Symphony Orchestra; Dorrance D. Roderick, organizer and long-time president of the Symphony; Mr. and Mrs. Maurice Schwartz, Miss Ann Bucher, Mr. and Mrs. Karl Goodman, Mrs. Sam Watkins, the Lochausen family, Pearson Wosika, the Sam Youngs, the Rev. B. M. G. Williams, Bishop S. M. Metzger, Mr. and Mrs. Joe Goodell, the Edward Heids and the Joe Heids, the Kelly sisters, whose parents, Mr. and Mrs. C. E. Kelly, were admired and loved by Mrs. Fox, Severo and Capitola Gonzalez, Mrs. Margaret Schuster Meyer and others.

4 List supplied by Mrs. C. R. McDaniel of Harding-Orr-McDaniel Funeral Home.

Few persons knew of Josephine's charitable gifts. Notations have been found of her gifts at the end of 1965. They include $1,128 to El Paso Symphony; $5,000 to Hotel Dieu School of Nursing; $1,000 to Salvation Army; $500 to United Fund and donations in amounts from $25 to $300 to thirty other churches, schools and charities or a total of more than $11,000 in donations.

For many years Glenn Bixler was her accountant. He and Mrs. Bixler had two sons, Glenn and Bruce, the former being a minister of a Presbyterian church in El Paso, and the latter, an accountant, who took over the account of Mrs. Fox after his father retired. Mrs. Fox was fond of the boys and her donations always included a check for the Rev. Glenn Bixler's church.

The subject of Josephine's religion has been a matter of interest and discussion among her friends and acquaintances. The fact is that she became a Catholic while in the hospital during her last illness. She asked Monsignor Lawrence Gaynor to baptise her and receive her into the church, which he did.

Bishop of El Paso, Sydney M. Metzger, says he was somewhat surprised at her decision, for although he had known her for many years and called on her from time to time in the hospital, he had never tried to convert her and did not know of her desire to enter the church. "Of course, there was not much opportunity for instruction," he said, "because she was very ill. But she was in complete command of her senses and knew definitely that this was what she wanted to do." Bishop Metzger said that although Josephine did discuss spiritual matters with him at times throughout the years he knew her, their visits were not confined to that. He recalled that she invited him to her home one time to see her antiques and art objects about which they had talked. "It was really quite a sight, that house," he said. "When I walked in, I thought it looked more like a shop than a home, there were so many things displayed in it."

Josephine is reputed to have told a certain friend that she went to the Bishop's home for tea one time several years ago and that "it cost me $50,000." Asked about this story, the Bishop's eyes twinkled and he said he knew of no such circumstance, that he certainly did not ask her for a donation. Then, reaching back in his memory, something came to him that might explain it. He said that the church bought a piece of property from Josephine for which they had an intended use, and she sold it to them cheap. He said he told her then that it was worth a great deal more than she asked. She said, yes, she knew it was, "but I want to do this for the church. I shouldn't make a profit on it from the church." So the transaction was completed. "Perhaps she figured that she lost that much money on the property," Bishop Metzger said, "by selling it to the church."

The fact that Josephine did not leave any property to the church in her will was introduced into the conversation. "In a way, it is better, I think," said the Bishop, "at least I cannot be accused of going to see her just to get her money. Not that the church couldn't use it," he continued, "but my motives and those of the other priests who went to see her would have been questioned had she changed her will in favor of our church."

For many years Josephine was a member of the congregation of First Presbyterian Church when the Rev. Paul Newton Poling was pastor there. Dr. Poling left El Paso to work in other fields, but upon returning in 1963 after an absence of seventeen years, he became chaplain at Providence Memorial Hospital. In 1964 when he found that Mrs. Fox was a patient, he remembered her as a former parishioner and began to include her in his round of calls. He said he would read scripture passages, say a prayer and visit with her for a while. She seemed to find comfort and be cheered by his visits. He asked her if she had left the Protestant faith, because he observed that Catholic priests and the Bishop were calling on her. She said, "Oh no," and he continued to call, doing so until her death.

From early childhood Josephine had known and loved persons of the Roman Catholic faith. She loved the Sisters who were her teachers as a little girl and they loved her. One of them, Sister Joseph, wrote Josephine through the years until she died in 1930. She longed to convert Josephine to the "true faith, so we can meet in heaven," she wrote.

Eugene Fox was a Catholic, though not devout. As Josephine thought about human mortality and the approach of death, perhaps she looked forward to a reunion with her Gene in heaven, and wished for the blessing of his church at the last. Who would care to ask through what portal she entered Paradise?

CHAPTER XVII

Epilogue

&ξ WHEN EL PASO NATIONAL BANK TOOK CHARGE as executors of the Fox estate, a young trust officer, Al Lawing, was designated to act for the bank. Mr. Lawing, astounded at the maze of collections in Josephine's home, arranged for a team of appraisers to come from Parke-Bernet in New York and make an appraisal of her personal property.

In the garage behind the Fox home, Al Lawing found two shiny black Cadillacs up on blocks. One, a 1918 model, had belonged to Allie Clardy; the other, a 1957 model, was the dream car which Josephine bought in New York and which was wrecked when she and Pietro Gentile started for California in it.

At the suggestion of Arthur Gale, a friend and former auditor for Mrs. Fox, the cars were driven downtown and placed on exhibit in the arcade of El Paso National Bank. Written bids were to be submitted for purchase. Many El Pasoans viewed the cars with a great deal of interest. Mr. Lawing said that it was surprisingly easy to get the 50-year old car out of the garage. "All we had to do," he said, "was drain the gasoline, blow out the cups and put in a new battery. Then we just drove it down the driveway."

When the auction was over, an El Paso dentist, Dr. John Dyal learned he had bought the 1957 model on his bid of $3,760.50. An antique car collector, J. C. Edwards of Milford, Connecticut, who happened to be passing through El Paso, saw the cars and made the high bid for the 1918 Cadillac. He bought it for $4,727.88.

After the appraisers had finished their work, Dr. Joseph Smiley, UT El Paso president, and Mrs. Smiley toured the Fox home and consulted with the executors about the removal of items to the University. Josephine's jewelry was placed in the vault of El Paso National Bank, and the dismantling of the house was begun.

The finest of the furniture, the rugs, paintings, art objects, silver and books were taken to the University, or put in storage until they could be placed at the University. It was realized then that many things remained to be disposed of. A member of the trust department of the bank suggested that the women of St. Clement's Episcopal Church, who were operating a successful thrift shop, be given the opportunity to sell these things. Mrs. Johnnie Spicer, chairman of this thrift shop (known as The Bargain Box) visited the Fox home with Mr. Lawing and was delighted with the idea of a sale. She said she thought it would be successful if they could hold it in the Fox home. and Mr. Lawing agreed.

Many days of preparation followed, with hundreds of items to be priced. Nothing was to be sold below the Parke-Bernet appraisal, the bank decided. Some of the Meissen and Dresden pieces remained, as well as period (but not highly valuable) tables, cabinets, chairs and lamps. There were fine light fixtures in addition to many whimsical items such as collectors dote upon. One volunteer worker was in charge of a large tray filled with a hundred door keys, souvenirs of the hotels at which Mrs. Fox had been a guest. The Episcopal women had taken the personal clothing and removed buttons, beading and laces, which provided delightful browsing for customers. Some fine linens were left for the sale, and other items such as shoes, cut-glass perfume bottles by the score, dozens of pairs of unused kid gloves and curiously enough, about a hundred unused cloth laundry bags!

On the designated morning of the sale, volunteer workers began arriving early and were surprised to find would-be customers waiting on the sidewalk. Before all workers were inside and ready for the 10 a.m. opening, the numbers outside had grown remarkably. Three and four abreast, they were queued up down to the corner and into the next block. They paid the fee as fast as St. Clement's chairmen, Mrs. Walter Driver, Johnnie (Mrs. Robert) Spicer or Mrs. Lewis P. Walker Jr. could accept it.

The sale had been announced for Saturday, Sunday and Monday. But so many people came on Saturday that almost everything was sold and not much stock remained for the other two days. But still people came, roaming through the house, admiring the fine marble mantels and the mahogany panelling of some of the rooms. They traipsed through upstairs rooms, where Mrs. Fox had really lived, looking at the "hat room" which had been filled with hundreds of picture hats stored in boxes that were stacked to the ceiling. However, the hats were not there for the sale, as they had been given to the costume department of the University Drama department. The hats are part of the legend of Mrs. Fox, who rarely appeared without a beautiful wide-brimmed hat.

Of interest to the curious were the two kitchens, one on each floor. In the downstairs kitchen were three ovens, an electric, a gas and a microwave, the latter said to be the first one installed in a private home in El Paso. When Josephine bought it, perhaps she planned to hire a cook, for she herself never learned to cook on any of the stoves.

When the doors had closed after the sale, Mrs. Spicer and other workers were on hand to wind up last details, when a couple came and asked to be admitted. In the city temporarily, they admired and immediately bought a pair of standing lamps at $150 each, which had failed to appeal to El Pasoans. This couple, who reside in Europe, were taking them to their home across the ocean.

One woman who had made some purchases of furniture, arrived with a pickup truck in which to haul her treasures away. But she carried clutched to her heart, the most treasured thing, a lovely black lace parasol. On her face was a look of enchantment, as if she imagined herself an elegant lady of a bygone era, riding through the streets of Paris in a carriage while holding the lace parasol daintily above her head.

After everything had been carted away, the several dozen women from St. Clement's who had been working hard for many days went home tired but happy. The sale had been a great success. The coffers of the University had been enriched; also the church women had made enough money to buy a bus for the young people of St. Clement's and to give aid to children in the church mission.

A few weeks later the house itself was sold to a neighbor, Manuel Vargas, who had long admired it. He said his daughter would make it her home. Actually it became a rooming house.

Al Lawing had moved away from El Paso in the meantime and Alfred Gardner had succeeded him in handling the Fox estate for El Paso National Bank. One of the last transactions, except for some real estate, was the sale of Josephine's jewelry. It had been decided to sell it all in one lot to the highest bidder. A few El Paso firms considered it, but most wanted to buy only some of the finer pieces. It was sold

November 23, 1971, to Terrell and Zimmellman, Inc., of Los Angeles, whose bid of $28,000 was the highest received.

James E. Rogers handled rentals of the estate property for the executors, and Errett Cummings, real estate officer for The University of Texas System, was in charge of real estate sales. Gross value of the estate according to the inventory filed in the County Clerk's office was $3,102,651.16.[1]

[1] El Paso *Herald-Post*, April 27, 1971.

ACKNOWLEDGEMENTS

M Y A I M in this biography has been to present Josephine Clardy Fox as a human being, approaching her life story in a factual yet sympathetic way, acknowledging but not emphasizing her foibles and eccentricities. I knew her over a span of more than twenty years, from about 1948 to the time of her death, but it was not a close relationship. However I did know well many of her friends, and having talked with them during those years and in more detail after her death, I have ventured to fictionalize occasionally in an effort to recreate her words and thoughts. The main outlines of her life history are firmly founded on authentic facts, as are those of her husband and parents.

I am dedicating this book to my husband, Earl Staples Burns, in gratitude for his patience and long suffering during the time it was being produced.

Persons at The University of Texas at El Paso have been most helpful and to them I extend my gratitude. Foremost among these is Dr. Joseph R. Smiley, who as president commissioned me to undertake the work and who, through the long months of research, exhibited a most genuine interest. I am deeply grateful to Dr. C. L. Sonnichsen, author of many books and distinguished professor of English at the University until his retirement in 1972, for his helpful advice and criticism. In Archives, Leon Metz, Bud Newman and Mildred Torok assisted in every way possible while I pored over the hundreds of letters and papers left by Mrs. Fox. Buried in these papers were many essential facts of her life history. To Carl Hertzog, who came out of retirement to design the book, my eternal gratitude; and to his able successor at Texas Western Press, Haywood Antone, go my thanks also. Centennial Museum director Rex Gerald and his staff assisted when needed.

Acknowledgement is made to the Missouri Historical Society for material obtained in its library in St. Louis and to the reference department of St. Louis Public Library where the author pursued biographical research. In obtaining material on the Desloge relatives in St. Louis, I am indebted to a cousin of Mrs. Fox, Joseph Desloge, for his letters, and to his widow and his secretary, Mrs. Frances Winters, for assistance after his untimely death.

So many El Pasoans have been helpful that it would be impossible to name them all, but a few will be mentioned. It seems that Mrs. Fox had almost become a legendary figure before her death despite, or perhaps because of, the seclusion in which she lived. Joseph M. Moreno, senior vice president of El Paso National Bank, granted me many interviews and gave invaluable insight into the later years of Mrs. Fox. During those years he acted as advisor, friend and secretary to the ill woman. Trust officers at the same bank, Al Lawing and later Al Gardner, who handled the estate, extended every courtesy and kindness.

The first chapter is based on material furnished by Jane Davis McMaster, wife of Major Richard K. McMaster. The chapter "Era of Elliott" is based largely on material provided by Norma Elliott, widow of Bill Elliott. Early in the research, I talked with Margaret Branch, the nurse who was with Mrs. Fox for many years and who helped arrange her funeral. Also in the early stages I received help from Mrs. C. N. Bassett; Mrs. Frances Vance Durling; Mrs. Jess Boykin; the late Mrs. Hugh White; Maria Martinez Pennington; Woodruff Lochausen and his sister, the late Mildred Lochausen Myles; George Matkin, board chairman of State National Bank; Dr. L. C. Feener and the late Dr. Stephen Schuster.

Highly valuable information about Eugene Fox and his railroad activities was received from Miss Erin Middleton, and other facts in this area were supplied by Mrs. W. C. Barnes. Stories about Josephine and her mother in the depression years are legion, but special light on that era was provided by two sisters of Grover Smith, Miss Juanita Smith and the late Mrs. R. M. Shaver. Members of early-day El Paso families who contributed much general information include Colbert Coldwell, Jane Burges Perrenot, Chris P. Fox, Mrs. Maurice Schwartz, W. S. Warnock, Mrs. Dexter Mapel, Mrs. James Hill (the former Aline Hague), Mrs. Terry Allen, Mrs. John Neff, Miss Margarita Gomez, Mrs. Florence Cathcart Melby, Mrs. Margaret Schuster Meyer, Robert T. Hoover Jr. and Jack McGrath.

Helpful information about Josephine's collections came from Mrs. Melby, Byron Merkin, John Rogers, Mrs. Durling and others in El Paso; from interviews with Carl Wright and B. F. Cass, both of Dallás; and by letters from former El Pasoans, John and Rena Gillett of Laguna Beach, California. Information about insurance and properties was generously given by Miss Betty Rogers and her father, James E. Rogers. Certain legal information was received from R. H. Feuille and from Eugene Smith. Among others whose help is acknowledged are Mr. and Mrs. Tom Lea, Mrs. Sherod Mengel, Marshall DeBord, Arthur Gale, Carl Beers, Pearson Wosika, Mrs. Luis Zork, Mrs. Reginald Fisher, Raymond Dwigans, Dorrance D. Roderick, Bishop S. M. Metzger and Dr. Paul N. Poling.

RUBY BURNS

September 7, 1973

INDEX